How to Get Published in the Best Political Science and International Relations Journals

How to Get Published in the Best Political Science and International Relations Journals

Understanding the Publishing Game

Marijke Breuning

Professor of Political Science, University of North Texas, USA

John Ishiyama

Distinguished Research Professor of Political Science, University of North Texas, USA

Cheltenham, UK • Northampton, MA, USA

Published by
Edward Elgar Publishing Limited
The Lypiatts
15 Lansdown Road
Cheltenham
Glos GL50 2JA
UK

Edward Elgar Publishing, Inc.
William Pratt House
9 Dewey Court
Northampton
Massachusetts 01060
USA

Paperback edition 2022

A catalogue record for this book
is available from the British Library

Library of Congress Control Number: 2021943598

This book is available electronically in the **Elgar**online
Political Science and Public Policy subject collection
http://dx.doi.org/10.4337/9781839107511

ISBN 978 1 83910 750 4 (cased)
ISBN 978 1 83910 751 1 (eBook)
ISBN 978 1 80392 462 5 (paperback)

Printed and bound by CPI Group (UK) Ltd, Croydon, CR0 4YY

Contents

Boxes

Acronyms

AJPS	American Journal of Political Science (journal)
APC	Article Processing Charges
APSA	American Political Science Association
APSR	American Political Science Review (journal)
CPS	Comparative Political Studies (journal)
DA-RT	Data Access and Research Transparency
DOAJ	Directory of Open Access Journals
DOI	Digital Object Identifier
ECPR	European Consortium for Political Research
EGAP	Evidence in Governance and Politics (network and data repository)
FFP	Fabrication, Falsification, and Plagiarism
FPA	Foreign Policy Analysis (journal)
GSQ	Global Studies Quarterly (journal)
ICMJE	International Committee of Medical Journal Editors
ICPSR	Inter-university Consortium for Political and Social Research (data repository)
IF	Impact Factor
INASP	International Network for the Availability of Scientific Publications
IRB	Institutional Review Board
ISA	International Studies Association
ISP	International Studies Perspectives (journal)
ISQ	International Studies Quarterly (journal)
JCR	Journal Citation Reports
JCR	Journal of Conflict Resolution (journal)

JEL	Journal of Economic Literature
JOP	Journal of Politics (journal)
LaTeX	document preparation system (free software)
OA	Open Access
OASPA	Open Access Scholarly Publishers Association
OHRP	Office of Human Research Protections
ORI	Office of Research Integrity
PDF	Portable Document Format (electronic file format)
PLOS	Public Library of Science
PRX	Political Research Exchange (journal)
QCA	Qualitative Comparative Analysis
R&R	Revise and Resubmit
RCT	Randomized Controlled Trials
SPSS	Statistical Package for the Social Sciences (statistical software)
SSCI	Social Science Citation Index
STATA	Contraction of "statistics" and "data" (statistical software)
TRAX	Transparency Appendix
WCRIF	World Conferences on Research Integrity Foundation

Introduction: how to use this book

The process of getting published in a peer-reviewed academic journal in political science or international relations can appear mysterious to scholars who are relatively new to the "publishing game." More seasoned scholars have often learnt about the process through trial and error, with occasional advice, and much frustration along the way. Although there is no foolproof strategy for getting your work published on the first try, understanding the publishing process should make navigating it less frustrating. The better you understand the publishing process, the more efficiently you can target your manuscript to journals at which it will have relatively good odds. It also allows you to better navigate communications with editorial offices, as well as develop a strategy for overcoming the disappointment associated with the inevitable rejection letters. Given the increasing pressure on emerging and early career scholars to publish – not only to advance their careers but also to land a first academic position – it has also become more important than ever to learn to navigate the publishing process as efficiently as possible. This book endeavors to make it easier for emerging and early career scholars to make a successful start in navigating the publishing game.

The above implies that journal articles have become the standard format for sharing the results of research in political science and international relations. Indeed, journal articles have attained an increasingly central position in academic publishing. Many universities are keen to have faculty publish articles in academic journals. Career advancement often depends in good measure on the ability to do so. Although journal articles have in many ways become the "gold standard" of publishing, books continue to be valued as well. However, it is now more common to publish journal articles in the earlier stages of one's academic career and produce books only at a later stage – usually in addition to, rather than as a replacement for, continued journal article publication.

To facilitate success in journal article publishing, this book endeavors to answer the many questions that emerging and early career scholars have about the journal publishing process. Some of these questions are likely to be practical ones. Others will pertain to bigger and broader questions, such as the question suggested by this book's title: *How do you get published in the best political science journals?* That question is not so easy to answer, as it requires consideration of the fit between the manuscript and the journal, as well as the audience you seek to reach with your work. We address both this larger question about the publishing game and more practical matters. Our goal is to demystify the process of publishing in peer-reviewed academic journals. We discuss what happens "behind the veil" at the editorial offices of journals, because we believe that a better understanding of what editors do will help emerging and early career scholars increase their likelihood of success in publishing journal articles.

There is surprisingly little guidance on the academic journal publishing process in political science and international relations, although there are many excellent books on writing and research (e.g., Powner 2015; Roselle and Spray 2016; Goodson 2017; Belcher 2019). Such books have an important part to play in your publishing success. They are indispensable for improving your writing and research skills. This book is not intended to replace such guidance. Instead, this book serves as a complement: we are convinced that it is easier to become successful in the publishing game if you also understand how the publishing process works. This book offers insight into that process.

What you find in these pages is based on our experiences with the journal publishing process as both scholars and editors. As scholars, we have experience publishing our own work. As editors, we have built expertise serving in multiple editorial roles for different types of journals. Our experience includes most recently the editorship of the *American Political Science Review*. John Ishiyama served as editor-in-chief, while Marijke Breuning served as an editor during the same time period (2012–16). In 2005, John Ishiyama became the founder and inaugural editor of the *Journal of Political Science Education* (JPSE). Marijke Breuning served as an editor of JPSE as well and we both remained editors of JPSE until 2012. Marijke Breuning further served on the inaugural editorial team of *Foreign Policy Analysis* (2005–09). Our first experience with editorship was as the joint book reviewer editors for *International Politics* (2000–03). In addition, we have both served on a number of editorial boards, reviewed numerous manuscripts, mentored many students and junior colleagues, and dispensed advice on "how to publish" in a variety of professional settings.

This book grew out of the realization that the advice we were able to provide in these various settings could only reach those who were able to attend – and the scholars attending such sessions often had many more questions than there was time to discuss. Therefore, we sought a way to broaden access to information about the publishing process and provide a resource that can be consulted as questions arise. The book serves in part as a "how to" manual that outlines step-by-step the various aspects of the publishing process, but we also address several issues of increasing importance in political science and international relations. We address the latter because publishing success is also dependent on understanding these issues. Where we can, we provide clear advice. However, in many instances, determining the best decision requires carefully taking into account the relevant circumstances. In such cases, we discuss the issues to consider and the currently acceptable practices. Where we cannot offer a simple recipe, we invite you to engage thoughtfully with difficult questions and tradeoffs.

WHAT YOU WILL FIND IN THIS BOOK

In Chapter 1, we provide a basic overview of the publishing process, discuss how to decide where to submit your work, when to submit it, and the value of a good abstract. Further, we discuss strategies for sustained productivity and guidance regarding co-authorship. This chapter lays the foundation for the remainder of the book.

Chapter 2 discusses what happens in the editorial office. We discuss the initial editorial screening, the review process and the decision process. These aspects of the publishing process are often shrouded in mystery, and misconceptions abound. Explaining these aspects of the process helps to understand why the review process takes time and why the outcome can be somewhat unpredictable. We provide some guidance as to when to contact an editor if the process seems to take unusually long. We also discuss the process of revising your manuscript, both in response to an invitation to revise and resubmit, as well as after a rejection. The chapter further describes the process that follows after your paper has been accepted.

Chapter 3 moves on to a discussion of ethics and integrity in publishing. Although important, most scholars in political science and international relations receive little training in these important aspects of research and journal publishing. The chapter includes a discussion of different forms of plagiarism as well as ethics surrounding human subjects research.

We follow this in Chapter 4 with a discussion of research transparency. This is an increasingly important subject in academic publishing. The chapter addresses it both regarding qualitative and quantitative scholarship in the discipline. It also discusses the difference between reproducibility and replication.

In Chapter 5 we discuss newer developments in academic publishing and focus especially on open access publishing. The publishing model that is most familiar in political science is one where publishing houses charge the end-user, i.e., the library or the individual who subscribes to the journal. Authors do not incur any costs. An emerging new publishing model is one in which the end-user has open access to the content of the journal and the publisher collects an article processing fee from the author. This model is used by some credible academic publishers, but also by predatory journals. The latter prey upon unsuspecting scholars and charge them to publish, usually after a very questionable or non-existent review process. Such publishing harms a scholar's academic reputation far more than enhancing it. We therefore think it is important to learn to distinguish such outlets from credible academic publishing opportunities.

We close the book with Chapter 6, which discusses some ways in which you can maximize the impact of your scholarship, the value of serving as a reviewer for academic journals, and maintaining consistent scholarly productivity over time.

Several chapters contain boxes that summarize information for quick review, or provide checklists or links to additional resources. We hope that these features make the book useful not only to learn about the publishing process but also as a quick reference guide to consult as you work to get published in the best political science journals.

1.   The publishing process

The journal article publishing process can seem opaque to those not yet familiar with it. However, it tends to follow a fairly predictable trajectory. Developing an understanding of the publication process is helpful for scholars. It will make it easier to navigate the process and become successful at publishing in well-respected journals in political science and international relations.

This chapter outlines the basic article publishing process and discusses several closely related issues – such as choosing a journal, how to judge whether a paper is ready to submit, sustaining publication over time, and co-authorship. The emphasis in this chapter is on the research article, which is the most common type of manuscript scholars in political science and international relations submit to academic journals. In later chapters, we will address different publication formats, such as research notes, review essays and book reviews.

Here, we provide a bird's-eye view of the publishing process. Issues that we do not address here, or mention only briefly, will be addressed in later chapters.

1.1   BASIC OVERVIEW OF THE PUBLISHING PROCESS

The trajectory from manuscript to published article follows a fairly predictable pattern. It generally involves several distinct steps. Although there will be some variation between academic journals and editors (or editorial teams) in political science and international relations, the publishing process tends to be quite similar across them. This means that it is possible to describe the article publishing process in general terms.

Once you have a manuscript ready for submission and have chosen a journal, the next step is to submit it. Most academic journals employ an electronic submission system. Quite a few journals use either *Manuscript Central* or *Scholar One*, but there are a number of other systems in use as well. Before clicking on the link to the chosen journal's submission system, check to make sure you have everything you will need.

Where do you find out what materials the journal requires? Journal webpages usually have a section that is entitled something like "author guidelines" or "instructions for contributors." There, you will find information on the maximum word count for research articles and other types of pieces the journal publishes – such as research notes or book reviews. Some journals publish only research articles, but others offer a variety of contributions. Make sure to check the information that pertains to the type of contribution you plan to submit.

The author guidelines not only include information on the maximum word count for the article, but usually also list a maximum word count for the abstract that should accompany the manuscript. The guidelines will specify whether the total word count includes the abstract, tables and figures, notes and the reference list. In addition, the guidelines provide information – and frequently examples – regarding the journal's citation and reference style, and whether tables and figures should be placed in the text, at the end of the manuscript, or in a separate file. Make sure that your manuscript conforms to these guidelines. Some journals will gladly review manuscripts that are not formatted in their style, but others will return or even desk reject them.

Other things you may need during the submission process include keywords that describe the subject matter of your manuscript, a short biography, names and contact information for suggested reviewers – or those you oppose – and a cover letter. Keep the cover letter short. Editors generally spend very little time reading such letters and will quickly move on to the abstract to get a sense for the paper. Because a good abstract is important, we will discuss this in a separate section later in the chapter.

Think carefully about the keywords that best capture the subject matter of your manuscript. The editor may look at the keywords to decide where the manuscript "fits" in terms of its subject matter and, therefore, who might be well-positioned to review it. In addition, the keywords are often printed below the abstract and are used to make your article accessible through various search engines.

In subfields of political science and international relations that intersect with economics, some journals will ask authors to provide the JEL code. This classification system was developed by the Journal of Economic Literature and has become a standard method for classifying scholarly contributions in economics. The intersection of the classification system with subjects in comparative politics and international relations is evident in some of the subcategories under "international economics": there are classification codes for, among others, "international conflicts," "international organization" and "postcolonialism." These codes are used like keywords and a number of journals use them in combination with keywords. Authors may choose multiple classification codes to describe their manuscript. If the journal to which you plan to submit your manuscript uses JEL codes, you can determine the most appropriate ones by checking the comprehensive "JEL Classification Codes Guide" offered by the American Economic Association (www.aeaweb.org/jel/guide/jel.php).

The biography can be a very short statement identifying you, your position and institutional affiliation, and possibly research interests and publications. The guidelines occasionally specify what must be in the biographical statement, but at other times guidelines only mention that you must submit one. In the latter case, consult a recent issue of the journal to identify the type of biographical statement that the journal employs. Model your own biographical statement after those published in the journal.

Suggested reviewers should be individuals who know the relevant literature and can evaluate your work fairly. Early career scholars often suggest the "big names" in their area of inquiry. This is seldom helpful, because such scholars get lots of requests to review – and the editor can probably think of them as well. Never suggest your dissertation advisor or committee members, as it would be a conflict of interest for any of them to review your manuscript.

A smart strategy is to suggest scholars you may have met when presenting your work at a conference. If they found your work interesting and you had a positive interaction with them, they may provide good feedback as reviewers as well. Do not worry too much about the rank and affiliation of the scholar you suggest, but instead focus on whether the individual has relevant expertise. Editors are always looking to expand their pool of qualified reviewers. They welcome suggestions that introduce them to scholars they may not have previously considered but who are clearly qualified to review the manuscript. Editors will not always use your suggestions. In some cases, the suggested reviewer may have already accepted a request to review for the same journal or completed one very recently. Editors usually make an effort to space out review requests to the same reviewer and try to avoid asking the same reviewer more than once or twice a year. In other cases, the editors do invite the suggested reviewers, but one or more of them declines to review the manuscript – something we discuss in more detail in Chapter 2.

It can be a bit tricky to oppose reviewers. Do this only if you can provide a compelling reason why a specific scholar should not be invited to review your work. For instance, if you know a possible reviewer to be extremely hostile to the theoretical or methodological approach your work represents, you can communicate to the editor that you believe that this individual is unlikely to provide a fair and unbiased review for this reason. The same may be true if there has been personal hostility and you think that the reviewer may be able to identify the manuscript as your work – for instance, because they are familiar with your research agenda or have seen you present a previous version of the manuscript. That said, you should not oppose a reviewer lightly. Differences of opinion – even strong ones – do not automatically preclude the capacity to provide a fair review. Indicate opposition to a reviewer only if you are quite certain that the person is sufficiently hostile that the paper will not receive a fair and unbiased assessment. To determine whether you should voice opposition to a specific reviewer, it is good to obtain advice from one or more trusted colleagues who can help you arrive at a well-considered decision.

After you have consulted the guidelines and have all the items you need gathered together – the brief cover letter, the anonymized manuscript in the style required by the journal and with any tables and figures in the required format and place, the abstract, keywords, biographical statement, and any appendices as separate documents – click on the link to the journal's submission system and follow the instructions provided. You may need to register for an account, provide some biographical data, and certify that the manuscript represents original work and is not under review elsewhere, before being directed to upload the various items. In most cases, the manuscript, tables and figures, and appendices require a file upload and the system will specify what type of documents can – or cannot – be uploaded (e.g., Word, LaTeX, PDF). In some cases, the cover letter is a file upload and at other times it is pasted into a window provided in the submission system. The abstract and the keywords are usually also pasted into windows. Submission systems vary in terms of the order in which documents are uploaded or pasted into windows, so follow the step-by-step instructions. Most systems will prompt you if you forgot to enter or upload something. Most also require you to review a PDF or html document that the system builds before you hit the final "submit" button. Be sure to look over the document to make sure this is the version of the manuscript that you want the editors to see.

After you have completed the submission process, the editorial office takes over with the review process. During the time your manuscript is under review, there is not much you can do besides wait. In Chapter 2, we will discuss what to do when the review process takes inordinately long. To be able to monitor this, you will want to keep a record of the date you submitted the manuscript. In most cases, the journal will send you an email notification that the paper has been received and/or has been assigned a manuscript number. Make sure to note this information and use the manuscript number in any correspondence with the editorial office.

Once the review process is complete, you will receive a letter from the editor that communicates and explains the decision. You will also receive two or more reviews. The editor may tell you that the manuscript has been rejected, that you are invited to revise and resubmit it, or that it has been (conditionally) accepted. It is quite rare for academic journals in political science and international relations to accept a manuscript after the first round of reviews. Rejections are very common. Invitations to revise and resubmit are to be celebrated. We will explore the review and decision process in more detail in Chapter 2, where we also address what happens subsequent to acceptance of the manuscript.

1.2 WHICH JOURNAL? (HOW TO CHOOSE A JOURNAL)

How do you decide where to send your manuscript? This decision can be agonizing, because you may submit your manuscript to only one journal at a time. Only after one journal has rejected your manuscript can you submit it to another journal. The review process that takes place between the moment you submit the manuscript and receipt of the decision letter is described in Chapter 2. For now, what is most important is that a number of months will elapse between submission and decision. A negative decision requires that you start the entire process anew at another journal. It is not difficult to see that several negative decisions can lead to a significant delay in getting a paper published.

To give your manuscript the best possible chance to move towards publication more quickly, do a little research to identify suitable journals for the manuscript's subject matter and methodology (Van Cott 2005; Polsky 2007; Rich 2013; Belcher 2019). Rather than simply sending every manuscript to the "best" or most prestigious outlet, carefully consider the fit between the manuscript and the journal. We do not suggest that you ignore information about the prestige of journals, but recommend that you use this information judiciously.

There are thousands of journals in political science and international relations (*Ulrich's Global Serials Directory* 2020). Indeed, there are many more journals than most advanced students and scholars in the discipline are able to identify. Most focus on a small subset of all existing journals and, even then, not all are perceived as equally attractive outlets. To make informed decisions about where to submit your work for publication, it is useful to consider both prestige and fit. Prestigious journals are frequently identified as "better," but the fit between the manuscript and the journal's mission and scope must also be considered.

The prestige of a journal can be assessed in various ways (Craig et al. 2014). Within political science and international relations, there have been several attempts to rank journals according to the assessments of scholars (Garand 1990, 2005; Garand and Giles 2003, 2007; Garand et al. 2009; Phillips 2014). That is one way of evaluating prestige. However, the focus has shifted increasingly towards metrics that do not depend solely on the reputation a journal has developed on the basis of the subjective perceptions of scholars, but on the basis of something more tangible – such as the number of times articles published in the journal are cited. This measure is interpreted as an indicator of the impact the journal has on scholarship in the discipline. While this measure has its shortcomings, it is transparent. And it is easy to understand how rankings based on it are calculated.

The *Journal Citation Reports* (JCR) have become a broadly accepted metric of impact (Craig et al. 2014). It ranks journals across a large number of disciplines by calculating an Impact Factor (IF). The JCR arrives at the IF for a journal (for a specific year) by counting all the citations to articles published in the two years prior to the year for which the score is calculated. For instance, the IF for 2018 adds all citations to articles published in, e.g., the *American Political Science Review* (APSR) in 2016 and 2017. The citations may occur in any journal, including the journal for which the score is calculated. The total number of citations in 2018 to articles published in the APSR 2016 and 2017 is then divided by the total number of articles that appeared in that journal during those two years. The JCR reports 409 citations of a total of 105 articles, or an IF of 3.895 for the APSR in 2018. By itself, this number tells us little. However, it places the APSR near the top of the 225 journals in political science and international relations for which JCR calculates an IF. The scores for most journals vary somewhat from year to year, which affects the rank ordering for a given year. In evaluating the prestige of a given journal, it is therefore useful to evaluate its trajectory over several years and to look at its general placement among the journals in the discipline.

The JCR is by no means the only ranking system. Alternative and increasingly popular efforts to rank journals are Scimago (http://www .scimagojr.com) and Google Scholar (http://scholar.google.com). These two alternative rankings have the advantage of being freely available on the web, whereas the JCR is usually accessed through a library subscription. The scores produced by these alternative ranking systems differ from the JCR. Consider again our example of the APSR. The Scimago score for this journal for 2018 is 6.531, which places it slightly higher in this index than in the JCR. Scimago also calculates an equivalent to the JCR. Because it collects its own data and does its own calculation, the scores differ from those produced by the JCR.

Google Scholar uses a different metric, the h5-index. This is an h-index calculated over five years (hence, h5). It measures whether at least h articles published in a specific journal in the past five years were cited h times. The APSR has an h5-index of 58 for the period 2014–18, which means that 58 articles were cited at least 58 times over this five-year period. This places APSR in the top two political science journals – higher than in either the JCR or Scimago. This variation in the rankings across these indices derives from differences in the formulae used for calculation as well as the data sources used to count citations. Despite the variation in the precise ranking, these indices largely agree on the placement of journals in top, middle and lower tiers.

Lastly, there is Altmetrics (http://www.altmetric.com), which does not focus on citations, but instead evaluates a variety of online interactions. For instance, Altmetrics counts mentions of research articles on blogs, in tweets, the news, policy documents, and syllabi, as well as Facebook, Wikipedia, Google+, LinkedIn, YouTube and more. In doing so, it measures a different type of impact: articles may be widely discussed, but not cited by the authors of subsequently published articles. For instance, articles on pedagogical innovations, such as those published in the *Journal of Political Science Education*, may have tremendous impact on the teaching practices of political science faculty who read and share them, but not be widely cited.

It is not surprising, therefore, that a comparison of citation metrics and Altmetrics shows that the latter captures a different type of impact that has added value (Costas et al. 2015; Williams 2017). In other words, Altmetrics is not an alternative to the citation metrics discussed in the previous paragraphs. Instead, it is complementary and provides insight into a different type of engagement with research articles. It highlights that some work may not garner a lot of citations, but is newsworthy, widely read, discussed, used in policymaking, or has an impact on teaching practices.

This overview of metrics for evaluating the impact of journals and the research they publish is not exhaustive. It is meant to illustrate that these indices and metrics provide useful information, but should be used judiciously. They can provide comparative perspective on the relative prestige of various journals and on the types of impact your scholarship could have. In addition, you might target different types of journals to connect with various audiences.

Journals in political science and international relations differ in their purpose and target audience. There are a small number of "general journals" that publish articles in most or all specializations within the discipline, such as the *American Political Science Review*. There are also broad subfield journals, such as *American Politics Research, Comparative Political Studies*, or *International Studies Quarterly*. Other journals focus on narrower research agendas or on geographic regions. Examples are *Communist and Post-Communist Studies, German Politics, Human Rights Quarterly*, the *Journal of Modern African Studies, Pacific Affairs*, or the *Review of International Political Economy*.

General journals often aim to publish scholarship that offers – and evaluates – theoretical insights that are of interest to scholars in more than one subfield of the discipline. Editors of such journals usually look for manuscripts that make important theoretical advances or offer novel ideas. The subfield and more narrowly focused journals also publish theoretically informed studies, but the scope of such studies may be narrower and they may therefore be of interest primarily to scholars in the specific subfield or area of inquiry. The editors of the most prestigious subfield journals often look for similar features as the editors of the general journals: novel contributions. Other subfield journals appreciate theoretical framing, but are also interested in manuscripts that offer solid empirical contributions.

To better understand the category into which a specific journal falls, start by taking a look at its webpage (Belcher 2019). Most journal webpages have information that describes the publication's mandate. This segment may be called "about," "aims and scope," or "mission and scope." The description may be fairly general and somewhat vague, but will provide some initial insight into the kind of scholarship the journal seeks to publish. To get further information, look at some recent issues to get deeper insight into the journal's fit for your work (Rich 2013). A comparison of the "aims and scope" and recent content of several journals can help to determine how editors and editorial teams translate the relatively vague language of their journals' mandates into actual content.

That said, be mindful that editors make decisions only on manuscripts that were actually submitted. If certain aspects of the journal's mission are not visible in the journal's content, it is tempting to think that the editors must not care to publish work in that area. However, it is equally plausible that the journal has a dearth of manuscripts in a specific area of inquiry. If your manuscript fits that niche, the editors may welcome your submission. If you are unsure, a brief inquiry may help you evaluate whether the editors might be interested in your manuscript. Their response will usually carry the caveat that the paper will need to survive the double-blind peer review process, but it allows you to gauge whether the editors perceive the manuscript as within the scope of the journal's mandate.

Should you submit your manuscript to a general or a more specialized journal? Consider whether the paper speaks to a general theoretical concern or whether it is more narrowly focused. General journals tend to publish articles that the editors judge to be of interest to scholars who pursue a variety of research agendas, whereas journals focused on specific subfields or research agendas cater to more narrowly defined audiences. Hence, step one is to evaluate whether your manuscript is likely to be primarily of interest to scholars who pursue similar research or might be of interest to a broader audience. This is a judgment call. The review process allows the journal's editor and reviewers not only to weigh in on the merits of the manuscript, but also on its appropriateness for the specific journal to which it was submitted. The decision letter and reviews may suggest that the manuscript is better suited for a different journal. In deciding what type of journal to send your manuscript to, try to imagine how editors and reviewers might judge your manuscript. Use feedback received at conferences to help you evaluate the suitability of your manuscript for a specific journal, or ask trusted colleagues in the discipline and your area of specialization.

In addition to the above two considerations, consider whether the journal is a good fit for the methodological approach employed in your manuscript. A review of the journal's mission as well as some recent issues will help you evaluate whether the journal publishes only articles using only a specific (type of) methodology or is open to a variety of approaches. Some journals will state explicitly that they are open to work using a variety of methodological approaches, whereas others will indicate a focus on a specific type of scholarship.

Once you have narrowed down a short list of journals, it is a good idea to check with colleagues in your department and the broader discipline. There are two reasons to do this: colleagues may know whether a specific journal is likely to arrive at a decision regarding your paper within a reasonable amount of time or whether it has a reputation for being quite slow. These things change over time, so pay particular attention to more recent information. A reasonable timeframe is usually something in the range of three to four months, but some journals develop reputations for taking much longer.

Another issue is that some journals have a substantial backlog of accepted manuscripts, which may lengthen the time between acceptance and publication. Increasingly, journals mediate this problem by publishing articles online, ahead of assignment to a specific issue. An article published in this way – often referred to as "first view" or "early view" – is considered to be published and will be fully accessible to all of the journal's subscribers. The only things that change after assignment to a volume and issue are the page numbers and, possibly, the year of publication. A volume may consist of three, four, or more issues, and usually coincides with a calendar year. The page numbers of "first view" articles always start at 1, whereas an article assigned to a volume and issue starts with a higher number – unless it is the first article in the first issue of a volume. Depending on the backlog, an article may have appeared in "first view" in one year, but been assigned to a volume and issue published in a subsequent year. Either way, others will be able to find, read and cite your article after it is published on the journal's "first view" page.

Lastly, it is wise to check on the journal's publishing model. Some journals pay operating costs out of subscription fees, whereas others are "open access." The latter means that you or your library do not need a subscription to access the published content. Instead, authors pay a fee to have their accepted manuscript processed for publication. The details of these different publication formats, as well as the advantages and disadvantages of these different publishing models, are discussed in more detail in Chapter 5. A checklist for evaluating journals can be found in the link provided in Box 1.1.

BOX 1.1　THINK, CHECK, SUBMIT

A good resource to consult can be found at https://thinkchecksubmit .org/. This website provides a series of questions to help authors evaluate journals. It is especially useful in determining whether a publication meets professional standards or might be a predatory publication (as discussed in Chapter 5).

1.3　WHEN TO SUBMIT? (BETWEEN GOOD ENOUGH AND PERFECT)

It can be difficult to know when a manuscript is ready to be submitted to a journal. There are risks in both submitting a paper that is not quite ready and in waiting to perfect it too much. The first will lead to rejection, the second means the paper never gets out of the starting blocks and into the review process. A paper that is never submitted is not going to get published, so it is important to get your manuscripts out the door as soon as they are ready.

A good basic rule is to get some feedback on a paper before submitting it to a journal (Polsky 2007; Lebo 2016). Such feedback can be obtained in different ways. You might ask a colleague familiar with the area of inquiry, whether at your institution or elsewhere, to provide comments on the specifics of the paper's argument. Importantly, you will want such a colleague to focus on the intellectual merits of the paper and not the writing. Hence, before asking for such feedback, consult a book that provides guidance on writing to ensure that the manuscript is written according to the basic standards of academic journal writing. There are many such guides available. Belcher (2019) provides a lot of sound advice to help improve your writing and to edit your own work. Concise guides that aid in avoiding basic errors and improving structure are provided by Zigerell (2013) and Thunder (2004).

A good way to get comments from scholars with similar research interests is to present your work at a conference. If you participate in a traditional panel, there will be a chair, discussant, and several other paper-givers. It is customary to share your paper with all of these other scholars. Although most larger conferences now offer an online paper archive, it is still useful to send the paper as an attachment to the scholars on your panel with a brief message. Doing so makes sure that they each have a copy of the paper without having to dig around the paper archive, which saves them time. The discussant is tasked with providing feedback on all of the papers presented as part of the panel. Occasionally, a chair will also provide some feedback. The other paper-givers may not. However, you could ask them for feedback as their work is likely to have some commonalities with yours. This can be an effective strategy, especially if you have constructive comments to offer to your fellow panelists as well.

Another strategy is to ask other scholars who are scheduled to be at the conference (but who are not part of your panel) and who work on similar research questions if they would be willing to read and comment on your paper. Not everyone will accommodate such a request, but some will. You can start by sending a query accompanied by the paper's title and abstract. This strategy may also be beneficial if you are presenting a poster. By communicating with scholars from whom you would like feedback (and sending them a copy of the paper), you improve your chances of obtaining useful feedback.

Further, you can approach scholars you have met at previous conferences and who expressed interest in your work with a request for feedback. Again, not all will have the time, but some may be willing to provide some comments, especially if your paper builds on their work. These approaches all help you obtain feedback as well as connect with scholars in your area of inquiry.

We have not yet mentioned your dissertation advisor and the members of your dissertation committee. You should not hesitate to approach them to ask for feedback, although they may have seen earlier drafts if the paper is part of your dissertation research. We mention them last to highlight the importance of reaching out more broadly to obtain feedback from scholars who have not seen previous drafts of the paper. They will not judge your paper on the basis of progress relative to earlier drafts, are more likely to compare your paper to others they have recently reviewed for various journals, and judge your work in that context.

Use the feedback of a few people to make improvements to the manuscript. Sometimes comments reveal that something you thought was crystal clear is confusing to a reader – now you have an opportunity to clarify your argument. Sometimes comments reveal questions about your data or your methods – use the comments to make sure you explain as clearly as possible what data you used, how it was measured, and why you used the methods you employed. On occasion, feedback will prompt you to make deeper revisions – perhaps you need to tweak your theory to consider an element you had taken for granted or overlooked, add a control variable, or use a different methodology, or connect your case study more persuasively to your theory. Do what is feasible to improve the paper. On occasion, that means explaining that something is "beyond the scope of your argument" (i.e., you will not fully address it in the paper) or adding a note that a specific measure is not available or not adequate (and why).

Taking the feedback of colleagues seriously does not mean that you have to do everything they suggest. The previous paragraph has already indicated that you may not be able to implement some of the suggestions. Another issue is that well-intended suggestions may change the focus of the paper if you were to implement them. In such a case, you need to consider whether those suggestions enhance or detract from the contribution the paper seeks to make – and use or ignore the advice accordingly. You should neither slavishly follow all feedback, nor dismiss it wholesale. Carefully weigh the feedback and use it judiciously to sharpen the paper's argument.

Should you ask for additional feedback after revising the paper on the basis of a set of comments? That is a tough call. In some cases, a paper might benefit from some additional feedback. However, the feedback and revision cycle should not be an endless one. In most cases, after getting feedback from a few scholars and improving the manuscript on that basis, it is time to send it to a well-chosen journal. The reviewers are sure to have additional feedback for further revisions. Your aim is not to be accepted on first try – remember, this rarely happens – but to have a manuscript that is sufficiently compelling that the editor and reviewers are intrigued by it. You want them to be interested and engaged, and to be able to envision the manuscript as an article in the journal – provided you make some changes and add some clarifications. In other words, you aim for an opportunity to revise and resubmit.

1.4 A GOOD ABSTRACT HELPS THE MANUSCRIPT

It is not easy to write a good abstract, but it is also quite important to ensure that your manuscript is accompanied by an accurate and appealing preview. Unfortunately, many scholars treat the abstract as an afterthought and cobble it together by copying sentences from the introduction. Doing so runs the risk of selling the manuscript short in a variety of ways. This can not only affect readership and the accumulation of citations after publication, but also whether a reviewer chooses to accept the invitation to review and even the editor's selection of reviewers. It is worth expending effort on the abstract.

To see the value of a good abstract, consider how you use the abstracts that accompany published work. Most scholars who try to become familiar or keep up-to-date with work in a specific area of inquiry peruse the titles and abstracts of articles to determine whether to read them. In the process, they pass up articles that do not seem to connect with their research agenda. Some papers will be rediscovered later through citations of them in other work and are located through such a channel. However, there may very well be other articles with useful content that are passed up, because the abstract did not provide sufficient information to make the article's contribution and usefulness readily discoverable. Now, consider that others will be using the abstract of your article(s) in the same way. It is not difficult to see the value of a good abstract for making sure that those interested in the field of inquiry can identify the article's usefulness, read it, and cite it in their own work – thus making it part of the scholarly conversation and advancement of knowledge.

However, the importance of a good abstract starts well before the article appears in print. Editors use the abstract as a guide to the manuscript. Their initial, quick reading of the full paper will be colored by what they gleaned from the abstract. On the basis of the understanding thus achieved, the editor identifies and invites suitable reviewers. The invitation to review is usually accompanied by the title and abstract of the paper. This is most certainly the case for journals that use online submission systems, which are usually programmed to insert this information into the request to review automatically. Hence, potential reviewers can use this to decide whether or not to accept the invitation. Busy scholars will look at the abstract and, if it does not pique their interest or does not give a clear description of the paper, may pass up the task of reviewing. The more often this happens, the longer it will take to line up a sufficient number of reviewers – and the more likely it is that the paper is reviewed by scholars with a more tangential connection to its subject matter. Most editors invite first those reviewers they perceive as the most closely affiliated with the area of inquiry into which the paper fits. A good abstract can help those scholars to agree that the paper connects their own research agenda and get them interested in reviewing it.

So, what makes a good abstract? Some journals employ a formula and ask that authors specifically address the following four elements in their abstracts: objective, methods, results, conclusion. This can be broadened to include five or six: problem, objective, design and methods, results or findings, conclusion, with a sentence devoted to each of these elements (Belcher 2019). It is possible to add one additional sentence to position the problem (or research question) in its proper scholarly context, which would result in a six-sentence abstract (Powner 2015). Before you start writing it, make sure to check the maximum length allowed by the journal to which you plan to send the paper. Do not submit a 250-word abstract if the journal specifies a maximum of 150 words.

In addition to length, Belcher (2019) recommends the use of active language, present tense, and strong verbs. The latter are common in introductions and theory sections as well, e.g., argue, demonstrate, show. Powner (2015) suggests that the abstract is one of the few places in a professionally written journal article where it is appropriate to use the occasional "I" (or "we" for a co-authored paper) in order to draw a contrast between previous scholarship and your own contribution. Furthermore, it may be a good strategy to weave the keywords into the abstract. Belcher (2019) notes that many search engines access only the title and abstract of journal articles. Hence, inserting the keywords into the abstract enhances the discoverability of your work.

With so much weight placed on the abstract, it pays to spend the time to carefully craft it. Make sure that it presents not only information about the manuscript's core research question and the broader literature to which it contributes, but also briefly addresses the methodology employed, findings, and conclusions or implications.

1.5 FILLING AND EMPTYING THE PIPELINE (SUSTAINING PUBLICATION OVER TIME)

Publishing one time is good, because it provides experience with the entire process. However, scholars in political science and international relations build careers by publishing repeatedly and in a variety of journals. Although universities and other employers – within and across countries – vary in their requirements for career advancement, they almost invariably value (and reward) scholars with active research agendas and successful publication records. Therefore, the challenge is to sustain your efforts to get published repeatedly over time.

After you have hit the "submit" button for one manuscript, all you can do is wait for the review process to be completed. As mentioned, the amount of time this takes is variable and you will not know exactly when you will receive the decision letter. Generally, several months pass between submission and decision. Use this time to work on another manuscript. And if you submit that one before hearing back regarding the first paper, start work on a third. What is "downtime" for one manuscript is an opportunity to make progress on other work.

Staggering several projects in this way begins to fill your research pipeline with projects at various stages. Working in this way requires a mechanism to keep track of the various projects. Some scholars use a whiteboard in their office, but it is also possible to keep a file on your computer. Use whichever strategy makes sense for you and your work habits. The important thing is to keep track of all projects and their state of completion. This should include: (1) manuscripts under review and the date they were submitted; (2) papers that have been accepted for presentation at a conference and therefore have a due date for completion of a draft; (3) projects that are partially complete (data has been collected or research has been completed); (4) plans for future projects with potential data sources.

If a manuscript receives an invitation to revise and resubmit, it should become a high priority for completion (Lebo 2016). Such an invitation means that the editor, on the basis of the reviews, believes that the paper has potential and can be publishable with some additional work. Your manuscript now has a very good chance of being accepted for publication, provided that the editors and reviewers judge the revisions to be sufficiently responsive to their concerns.

If a paper has been rejected, make sure to send it to an alternative outlet quickly. Use the reviews to revise the manuscript. In this case, you need not respond to everything, but you will want to make those revisions that give the manuscript a better chance at the next journal. Chapter 2 will discuss these two scenarios in more detail.

Here, the important thing is to remember is that you need a mechanism to keep track of various projects. This makes it possible to use the time spent waiting on the review process for one manuscript productively to make progress on one or more other projects. That said, if you receive an invitation to revise and resubmit while in the middle of another project, it makes sense to set the other project aside to attend to the revisions first. In other words, try to use your time efficiently but also prioritize the papers that are closest to exiting the pipeline – those papers that with a little more work are most likely to become accepted manuscripts. After completing the revisions and returning the manuscript to the journal, you can pick up where you left off with the work you interrupted.

Working in this way, you will always have multiple projects at various stages of completion. You will also very likely have several papers under review simultaneously. Lebo (2016) recommends that you try to always have three manuscripts under review. Those could be initial reviews or papers sent back out after revisions. In our view, the number of papers you have under review at any one point in time is likely to vary, in part due to the somewhat unpredictable nature of the review process. Another factor that will affect how many projects you have in the research pipeline at any given moment is your job: if you are employed at a research university, you will need to have more projects in your pipeline at any one time to satisfy the demands for research productivity than if you are at an institution with a less intense focus on research. However, no matter where you are employed, scholars with active research agendas and successful publication records tend to advance in their careers more readily. While goals may differ depending on the requirements of your employment, try to have a pipeline with projects at various stages.

1.6 CO-AUTHORSHIP: WITH WHOM AND IN WHAT ORDER?

Getting published in journals in political science and international relations has become a less solitary endeavor over the past several decades. Co-authorship is increasingly common, as has been observed by a number of scholars (Fisher et al. 1998; Sigelman 2009; Lake 2010; McDermott and Hatemi 2010).

Multiple factors have contributed to this development. The availability of electronic communications has made it easier to collaborate, although the distribution of access to these technologies is geographically uneven. Some scholars (most often in the global North) can discuss research projects with one another in real time and on-screen, even if they are miles apart and in different time zones. Other scholars (especially those located in some parts of the global South) have less reliable access to electronic communications and may primarily communicate via email. Even then, access to electronic communications has made it easier for scholars who live on different continents to collaborate. In addition to technologies that permit real-time or speedily delivered communication, there are now multiple technologies for file-sharing – such as Google Docs (https://docs .google.com) or Dropbox (https://www.dropbox.com) – which make it easier for multiple authors to collectively write and edit manuscripts.

That said, collaboration is not distributed evenly across the different subfields of political science. Co-authorship is least common in political theory (or political philosophy) and most common among scholars engaged in quantitative research work (Fisher et al. 1998). In some cases, this is a function of the need to have multiple coders create large-scale datasets. The development of new datasets requires substantial labor and is often undertaken by teams of scholars, who then also perform the initial analyses of that new data and report them in co-authored, article-length manuscripts. In addition, as the statistical methods employed in a project become more sophisticated and specialized, it is more likely that scholarship has more co-authors, with each contributing identifiable expertise regarding a specific aspect of the collective project (Fisher et al. 1998).

This indicates that there are important reasons for co-authorship. First, joint effort makes larger-scale projects possible. Second, it brings together scholars with different kinds of skills and/or expertise. In both cases, it is important to consider what the various co-authors bring to the project (Van Cott 2005; McDermott and Hatemi 2010). If done well, co-authorship can lead to better and more innovative work than what any of the collaborators can produce alone. However, collaboration does not invariably yield better results. One study found that co-authored manuscripts submitted to a prestigious journal were not more likely to be accepted than single-authored ones (Sigelman 2009). Hence, if the likelihood of acceptance at a prestigious journal is taken as a valid measure of a manuscript's quality, then this study suggests that co-authored papers were not significantly better than single-authored ones.

Not all collaborations are equally successful. An important question to ask is: what do the partners expect from, and what does each bring to, the collaboration? Co-authorships are most likely to be fruitful when the partners bring complementary interests and skills to the project, are willing to discuss a reasonable division of labor between them, and deliver on their promises (McDermott and Hatemi 2010). If you engage in collaborations with different partners, your role in each project may be somewhat different, depending on the requirements of each one and the skills you and your co-author(s) bring to that project. There certainly is not one single way to successfully engage in collaboration. However, it is always important to make sure each scholar understands what the other(s) in the team expect of them from the project's inception and throughout to its final conclusion.

Productive co-authorships can take many forms. As a graduate student, collaboration with a faculty member can be a good way to learn about both the research and publication process. The faculty member may take an active role or may serve as a "senior author," who provides mentorship and guidance. At different career stages, you may benefit from different types of collaborations. Partnerships can be especially important in inter-disciplinary research, but they can also be productive when partnerships stretch across subfields, bring together knowledge of different literatures, or skills in different methodologies. In such cases, the research team collectively has a more expansive skill set than any one scholar who is a member of that team.

The products of collaboration require that scholars make difficult decisions about the order in which the co-authors will be listed. This is not a trivial question, although it is often sidestepped. An easy solution is to list co-authors in alphabetical or reverse alphabetical order. Indeed, this is the most common trend in co-authorship in political science and international relations, but it is seldom an accurate reflection of the co-authors' relative contribution to the manuscript (Fisher et al. 1998; Biggs 2008; Lake 2010).

Why does author order matter? Those who read published articles often make the implicit assumption that the author listed first must have made the more important contribution to the manuscript's content. This assumption has consequences. In economics, co-authored work cus-tomarily uses alphabetical order. In that field, scholars with surnames beginning with a letter that falls earlier in the alphabet are more likely to reap a variety of professional benefits (Lake 2010). This suggests that avoiding difficult discussion about author order is beneficial to those with early-in-the-alphabet surnames and detrimental to those with later-in-the-alphabet surnames. Hence, conversations about author order are important for equity among co-authors.

Unfortunately, political science and international relations do not have an established convention regarding author order. This means that collab-orators cannot refer to their discipline's convention to settle such matters. However, the evidence from economics suggests that the question is too important to avoid addressing thoughtfully. Indeed, Lake (2010) also notes that the avoidance of discussions about relative contribution actually underscores the importance of the issue. He suggests a sensible solution: include with the manuscript a short statement that details the division of labor among the co-authors. Such a statement can be brief. However, if published as an authors' note, it will provide an explicit and incontrovertible record of each co-author's contribution to the article. This will be important not only when the contributions differ, but also to underscore that they were equal. Box 1.2 provides some examples of statements authors might include to provide transparency regarding the roles of each of the co-authors in the production of the manuscript.

BOX 1.2 SAMPLE STATEMENTS OF CO-AUTHORS' RELATIVE CONTRIBUTIONS

- *Authors are listed J, B, and N.* The authors' note explains: Author J was primarily responsible for drafting this article. Author B collected the data and analyzed the statistical results. Author N was the senior author. Authors J and N shared equally in the origin and design of the project.
- *Authors are listed E, A, and W.* The authors' note explains: Author E conceived the project and is primarily responsible for drafting this article. Author A researched and wrote the case study on X. Author W researched and wrote the case study on Y.
- *Authors are listed R and D.* The authors' note explains: Author R is the first author of this article, which follows directly from her dissertation research. Author D is the senior author.
- *Authors are listed A, B, and C.* The authors' note explains: Author A, Author B, and Author C contributed equally to this article.

Source: Lake 2010 (modified).

The above implies that all co-authors had an identifiable role. However, this is not always the case. Both the inclusion of (an) author(s) who did not in fact make a substantial contribution and the failure to include a scholar who did make a significant contribution are considered forms of research misconduct (Albert and Wager 2003; Roig 2015). The first is called "gift authorship," which means that someone listed as an author did little or nothing to earn authorship. The second is called "ghost authorship," which means that the efforts of someone who made a substantial contribution to the research and writing of the manuscript are not acknowledged.

Albert and Wager (2003) describe two main reasons why gift authorship occurs. One, an author may invite a senior scholar as a co-author, thinking that this is expected. Two, an author may invite a colleague to be listed as co-author, even though the latter has not done any work, with the expectation that the colleague will return the favor and you both will enhance the number of your publications. Although the second reason is easily identifiable as unethical behavior, the first is more complicated to adjudicate. Consider, for instance, the situation mentioned above: a graduate student receives mentorship and guidance from a faculty member. The latter's mentorship role may have included discussions about the conceptualization and design of the project, as well as feedback on subsequent drafts. However, the faculty member has not participated in the data collection, analysis or writing.

Available guidelines suggest that the faculty member's co-authorship hinges on whether she or he has made "substantive" or "significant" contributions to the manuscript (Albert and Wager 2003: 34; Roig 2015: 44). Of course, what defines such a contribution is a judgment call. Both Roig (2015) and Albert and Wager (2003) reference the recommendations of the International Committee of Medical Journal Editors (ICMJE 2020), which provides detailed guidance regarding authorship. However, the ICMJE (2020) ultimately acknowledges that who qualifies as an author is best determined by the scholars involved in the research project. The ICMJE (2020) specifically states that this is not a matter for journal editors to adjudicate, but recommends that any disagreements regarding authorship should be settled by the institution(s) where the research was conducted.

The reverse of gift authorship is ghost authorship. The latter refers to a scholar who has made substantial contributions to a research project but is not listed as an author on the resulting publication (Albert and Wager 2003). This is also problematic. One, a scholar who has invested time and effort into a project deserves appropriate credit for their work. Two, by ignoring the contributions of one author, the remaining author(s) imply that they have played a greater role in producing the manuscript than they did. Here, too, the scholars involved in a research project are best positioned to determine who qualifies as an author (Albert and Wager 2003; ICMJE 2020).

To avoid disagreements, it is best to discuss both who will be included, as well as the author order, during the planning stages of a project and before starting to draft each article (Albert and Wager 2003). If the issue of authorship and author order has been discussed explicitly at the start of the project, it is also easier to revisit these issues in light of unanticipated changes in contributions. The bottom line: authorship and author order should be a fair reflection of the contributions made by each of the scholars involved in a co- or multi-authored project. Ultimately, those who are part of the research team are best positioned to determine who should be included and in what order. Hence, it is best to have those difficult discussions before you are confronted with a colleague's claim that they should have been included as an author.

2. The review process

After sending off the manuscript or – more commonly – clicking the "submit" button on your computer screen, the wait begins. What happens between submitting your manuscript and receiving a decision letter varies, because the processes and practices of editorial offices differ somewhat. We discuss both the common elements of the review process, as well as some of the variations.

This chapter lifts the veil to describe what happens in the editorial office. Insight into how manuscripts are processed and what is involved in securing reviews takes some of the mystery out of the publishing process. We include this information because knowing what happens between clicking the submit button and receiving the decision letter can help authors to better navigate the publication process. This chapter also addresses desk rejects and rejections after review, and provides guidance on how to handle those situations. Further, the chapter discusses decisions on how to deal with invitations to "revise and resubmit" and explains what happens after your paper is accepted.

2.1 INITIAL SCREENING AND "DESK REJECTS/ DECLINE TO REVIEW" – AND WHAT TO DO

After you submit your paper, the journal's editorial staff is notified by the web-based manuscript submission system. Alternatively, if the journal accepts submissions via email attachments, the editorial staff will log the manuscript into their database before they perform an initial screening of the paper. The initial screening includes several elements, all of which occur before your paper is officially under review.

In online submission systems, authors can check the status of their manuscript. If you see that a week or so after submission the paper is not yet under review, this means that the journal office is still working on the initial screening process. This is not cause for concern. The amount of time it takes to complete this initial screening varies, in part because the flow of manuscripts can be uneven. So, if a lot of authors submit manuscripts around the same time, some will have to wait a bit longer to be processed.

Who performs the initial screening depends on the journal, its staffing, and its customary workload. Well-established and prestigious journals that are sponsored by professional societies may receive over a thousand manuscripts per year. Such journals may have a permanent staff member at the association's office or at the university at which it is housed. Such a staff member is usually called the "managing editor," and this is the person tasked with the initial processing of incoming manuscripts. At well-established journals with very large numbers of submissions, the managing editor may supervise one or more editorial assistants, usually graduate students, who complete part of the initial screening process.

Smaller and newer journals tend to receive much smaller numbers of manuscripts annually – sometimes less than a hundred per year. Such journals may have no staff beyond a single editor. This means that all tasks, including the initial screening, are completed by that editor. Of course, many journals fall somewhere in between these extremes and may have a small staff – often one graduate student who assists the editor with the initial logging and screening of manuscripts.

Journals sponsored by professional societies and/or publishers often receive a stipend to offset the cost of hiring a managing editor and/or editorial assistant(s). As a way to save costs and use personnel more efficiently, some of these sponsors are now advocating the use of "virtual editorial assistants." Their job description is very similar to that of the managing editor or editorial assistant, but the work is performed remotely. One virtual editorial assistant may work for several journals and divide their time to work on each as needed, depending on the volume of submissions each receives.

Irrespective of the type of staff a journal has, the initial screening of the manuscript will consist of a "technical check" to make sure the manuscript has the appropriate format and length, and does not inadvertently identify its author. The review process of academic political science journals is intended to be "double-blind," which means that the author(s) do not know who the reviewers are, and the reviewers should not be able to discern the identity of the author. Editors usually want to make sure that the author(s) do not reveal their identity by writing phrases such as: "I argued in my earlier work (self-citation)" or "building on my earlier work (self-citation)." If the technical check turns up the use of such self-references, the paper will be returned to the submitting author to change the language surrounding such references.

The "submitting author" is a concept used most often in relation to co-authored manuscripts. The scholar who uploads the manuscript into the electronic submission system is referred to as the "submitting author" and correspondence between the journal and the authors is often directed only at the submitting author. The editor(s) will assume that the submitting author communicates with the other author(s). That said, some journals send the co-authors an automated message that asks them to confirm that they have agreed to be co-authors on the submitted paper.

In addition to requiring the elimination of self-references, editors may also ask authors to reduce the number or type of self-citations, even if those are not presented in a way that explicitly reveals the author(s). This is a judgment call. Some editors will ask that an author remove a reference to their unpublished dissertation. Such a reference, especially in work by an early-career scholar, could potentially reveal the identity of the manuscript's author. Other editors will be sensitive to the number of self-references an author includes. For instance, if there are seven references to earlier work by the manuscript's author and there are no more than two references to work by any other scholar, reviewers may suspect that the seven references to a single scholar's work indicate the identity of the author of the paper.

A last category of references that editors may ask to be removed are unpublished papers. Unless the paper is widely available through a working paper series or online paper archive, references to unpublished works can also signal the identity of the author. Again, editors may ask you to leave such references out of the manuscript to maintain the double-blind nature of the review process.

Not all editors pay equally close attention to these matters. However, you might consider eliminating references to a dissertation or unpublished papers, and limit the number of self-citations. Doing so avoids the likelihood that the editor sends the manuscript back and asks you to fix these issues, delaying the review process. After the manuscript has been accepted, there will be an opportunity to add such references – provided that you can do so while staying within the maximum word limit. Note that some journals offer some flexibility regarding word limits, whereas others strictly enforce them. The more competition there is for space in a specific journal, the more likely it is that its editor(s) will demand that you adhere to the word limit.

Policies regarding adherence to the journal's stylistic guidelines and manuscript length differ as well. Some editors will return a manuscript if it exceeds the journal's maximum word length, but not if it does not fully conform to the journal's guidelines regarding citation and referencing style. Others will return manuscripts that do not conform to the journal's referencing style – and indicate in their "guidelines for authors" that they expect submitted manuscripts to conform to these requirements.

As a general rule, it is a good idea to invest a little time to check on the journal's maximum word limit and style guidelines, and to make an effort to follow these instructions. This means that the manuscript uses in-text citations if that is what is specified, or footnotes if that is the journal's citation style. It is tedious to change a paper from one referencing style to another, but submitting it in the required style conveys that you are seriously interested in placing your work in the journal. Finally, make sure you check for grammar and spelling. Sloppy work does affect the judgment of editors and reviewers! Investing time in following the guidelines and editing your work also minimizes the risk that the editor sends the manuscript back for you to fix these issues before considering the manuscript further – or to reject it because the manuscript does not conform to length and style guidelines, or is sloppily written.

After the manuscript has passed the technical check, the managing editor or editorial assistant passes it on to the editor for an initial reading. If a journal is led by a team of multiple editors, either the lead editor (also called editor-in-chief) or the managing editor will assign the manuscript to one of them to shepherd it through the remainder of the review process. At some larger journals with multiple editors, each has a separate area of expertise and will generally – but not always – handle those manuscripts that fit into her or his area of expertise. In addition to expertise, journals with multiple editors also try to achieve an equitable distribution of the overall workload. This means that editors occasionally supervise manuscripts outside of their area of expertise. Hence, you cannot assume that your manuscript will be assigned to the editor with the closest expertise when a journal is edited by a team.

The initial reading determines whether the manuscript fits within the scope of what the journal publishes and will be reviewed. The editor may decide that the manuscript is not a good fit for the journal. As discussed in Chapter 1, always read the "aims and scope" statement of a journal before submitting your work. Doing so should avoid the most obvious situations of a poor fit. However, editors occasionally interpret their journal's mandate differently from your reading of it. In other cases, they seek to shift the journal into a new direction and decline to review papers in areas that used to be welcome in the past. Either way, despite your best efforts, it is not always possible to avoid this situation. An editor's decision to decline to review the manuscript is often referred to as a "desk reject," because the manuscript did not move beyond the editor's desk and into the review process.

Although it is unpleasant to receive the news that the editor has "declined to review" your manuscript, such a decision usually happens quickly and allows you to move on to another journal. Rather than waiting several months for the outcome of the review process, you can send the manuscript to another journal within days or weeks. The proportion of desk-rejected manuscripts varies between journals. The *American Political Science Review* (APSR), the *American Journal of Political Science* (AJPS) and the *Journal of Politics* (JOP) decline to review between 20 percent and 35 percent of submissions annually. For 2019, higher desk reject rates were reported by *Foreign Policy Analysis* (FPA) and *International Studies Perspectives* (ISP) – both around 40 percent. The rate at which manuscripts are rejected without review is not constant – it varies with editors (or editorial teams) and across time. Some years ago, *International Studies Quarterly* (ISQ) reported a desk reject rate of 45 percent, but this has declined to 35 percent in 2019.[1]

In addition to issues of fit, editors sometimes decline to review manuscripts that they judge to not have a very good chance of surviving the review process at their journal (Polsky 2007). Part of the reason to desk reject in such a case is that it can be difficult to secure a sufficient number of reviewers. Editors hesitate to ask scarce reviewers to spend time on papers that have an extremely low chance of surviving the review process. Sometimes, they will provide one or more suggestions for alternative outlets that they judge to be a better fit for the manuscript. In other cases, an editor may suggest some improvements that will give the paper a better chance at an alternative outlet. If so, use that information and research those outlets as you decide on the next journal to which to send your manuscript.

2.2 "WAITING FOR GODOT" – WHEN TO CONTACT AN EDITOR

The review process sometimes feels like an endless waiting game. As an author, the process can test your patience. Journals that use web-based submission systems usually enable you to go back into the system and check the "status" of your manuscript. This can be helpful, but also frustrating. It is useful to know a bit about what happens behind the scenes and how to interpret the information provided by the submission system.

If, after the initial reading, the editor decides to review the manuscript, the next step is to identify potential reviewers. Editors of well-established and prestigious journals may be able to rely on an editorial assistant – usually an advanced graduate student – to help identify potential reviewers. The editors of smaller journals usually must identify reviewers themselves. This is a difficult task. As an author, you can facilitate the search for appropriate reviewers by furnishing the names of one or more "suggested reviewers," if the journal's submission system provides the opportunity to do so – something we discussed in Chapter 1. Whether or not the editor actually invites these reviewers, the suggestions can be very helpful: the editor will better understand what sort of scholars you would view as fair judges of your work.

Some journals also provide the opportunity to let the editor know that you would prefer to avoid certain reviewers. This gives you the opportunity to let the editor know of any special considerations – such as vehement debates within a specific area of inquiry that lead some scholars to reject the work of those on the other side of that debate. The editor is not under any obligation to honor a request to avoid a specific reviewer. Depending on the editor's evaluation of the reasons you provide, she may or may not choose to abide by your request.

Once the editor has identified potential reviewers, she will approach them with a request to review your manuscript. Journals using web-based submission systems will usually include a copy of the paper's title and abstract with the request. Several things can happen at this stage: (1) the reviewer reads the abstract, finds it interesting, and agrees to review the manuscript; (2) the reviewer may or may not find the abstract appealing, but is swamped with other tasks and declines to review; (3) the reviewer never responds to the request. This can happen for a variety of reasons. While frustrating for editors, it does not always mean the reviewer has simply hit the "delete" button on the request; in some cases the reviewer's email address has changed, but the submission system was not updated and the request simply never reaches its destination. The bottom line is that editors must send out substantially more requests than the number of reviewers they need to be able to make a decision on the manuscript.

In the best-case scenario, several reviewers immediately agree and submit their review in a timely fashion. Most journals request that reviews be submitted within four weeks from the date the reviewer agrees to evaluate the manuscript, although many journals extended the review period to six weeks or more during the coronavirus pandemic in 2020–21.

During this time period, it was even more difficult to find reviewers, adding time to already lengthy review processes.

After a sufficient number of reviews has been received, the editor will need time to read them, reread the manuscript, and formulate a decision. Journals differ in the minimum number of reviews they require. Journals that are edited by a team of multiple editors may share their draft decision letters with one another and discuss decisions – especially if the proposed decision is a "revise and resubmit" or "accept." In other words, even when a full set of reviews has been submitted, you may not immediately receive a decision letter from the editor.

Note that web-based submission systems often indicate that the required reviews have been received when two reviews have been submitted. As an author, you may be under the impression that you should receive a decision letter any day. That may not be the case. Although some journals will make decisions on the basis of two reviews, others will wait for a third – and sometimes even a fourth. Some journals will reject manuscripts that have received two negative reviews, but will wait for additional reviews if the verdicts are mixed. This means that, depending on the editorial policy, there may be very good reasons why the editors are not making a decision – they may be waiting for the evaluation of one or two additional reviewers.

The amount of time consumed by the review process varies, in part because the best-case scenario often does not materialize. If the first set of scholars who have been invited to review the paper all decline or fail to respond, the editor must find alternative scholars to approach about reviewing it. This can be quite challenging, especially in smaller subfields where the pool of scholars with relevant expertise is smaller. Another reason for the variation in the length of the review process is that some reviewers agree to evaluate a manuscript and either take (much) longer than the requested four weeks to deliver their review or fail to deliver a review altogether, even after repeated queries by the editor.

Editors may do their best to complete the review process within a reasonable amount of time – which is customarily defined as about 3–4 months – but they are dependent on the voluntary service of reviewers (Polsky 2007). Reviewers do not get paid to review manuscripts for academic journals in political science and international relations, so editors have little leverage.

When is it acceptable to contact the editor about a manuscript that has been under review a long time? Given the difficulties editors may face in finding reviewers, it is not a good idea to contact the editor exactly 90 days after submitting the paper and demand that they respond right away. However, if the process gets closer to the four-month mark, it is fine to write a brief note to the editor to inquire about the status of the review process. Doing so is likely to accelerate the process. The editor is likely to check on the status of the review process for your manuscript. She may discover that it is time to send a query to a reviewer who is late in submitting an evaluation, that an additional reviewer needs to be asked, or find that a decision can be made. Even editors who monitor their submission system carefully occasionally let something slip and your polite query about the status of the review process can help mediate that.

2.3   THE DECISION PROCESS

Whether an editor makes a decision with two reviews or waits for additional ones, the process is similar. Most journals ask reviewers to provide written comments for the author(s), as well as a summary judgment. The latter usually offers the reviewers several categories – such as: reject, major revision, minor revision, accept – and requests that reviewers pick the one that best reflects their overall judgment of the manuscript. Additionally, reviewers can provide confidential comments that are seen only by the editor.

The summary judgments provide an initial impression, but are not very reliable. It is not uncommon for reviewers who largely agree on the merits of a paper to provide different summary judgments. One may suggest the paper be rejected, whereas another suggests major revisions. Alternatively, one may suggest the paper requires only minor revisions, whereas the other considers the same revisions major. In addition to using different labels for similar substantive judgments, it is also possible for reviewers to disagree fundamentally on the merits of a manuscript. Each judges the manuscript independently and it is not uncommon for two or three reviewers to focus on different aspects of the paper, often on the basis of their own expertise, and arrive at very different conclusions on the merits of the manuscript. For instance, one may focus on the theoretical advance made by the paper, whereas another may focus on the adequacy of the statistical method the author employed, or quarrel with information presented in a case study. With so many possibilities for variations in judgment, it is surprising how frequently a panel of reviewers is broadly in agreement.

The editor will carefully read the reviews, noting similarities and differences in the comments made by the reviewers. The editor will also read the manuscript to form her own judgment. If any of the reviewers made confidential comments to the editor, those may also influence the decision process. What sort of things would reviewers wish to communicate to editors but not to authors? In some cases, reviewers will convey that they have seen the manuscript before. This is not unusual, because the number of scholars who can adequately evaluate research on a specific research question may be fairly small. What they say in addition, however, can be important. If the reviewer states that they reviewed the manuscript for another journal, they may also indicate whether or not the author made any effort to revise it before sending it to the next outlet. If you made no changes and the reviews are mixed, the editor will quite likely decide to reject the paper. On the other hand, if the reviewer indicates that the paper has been much improved since she or he reviewed it for a different publication, the editor might perceive that as an encouraging sign. In this case, the editor might be more likely to take a chance on a paper with mixed reviews, because the author has demonstrated a willingness to respond to criticism.

After reading the reviews and the manuscript, the editor must consider whether recommended revisions are doable and whether the revised paper will be of interest to the journal's audience. Both are a judgment call. If the reviews all point in the same direction, the editor's job is easier than when the reviews are mixed. In the latter case, the reviewers may have rendered contradictory verdicts and comments. This situation requires very careful work by the editor: she must evaluate why the reviewers have such different judgments, whether aspects of these judgments can be reconciled and – most important– whether to give the author an opportunity to revise the paper. If so, the editor may feel compelled to provide some carefully worded guidance to help the author navigate between the different reviews.

If the reviews all point in the same direction, the editor has more solid footing. If the reviews all point towards rejection, the editor usually writes a brief decision letter. In the next section, we will discuss this scenario in more detail and provide some guidance on next steps.

The reviews may also collectively point in a more positive direction. Whether the requested revisions are minor or more extensive, the editor usually tries to provide some guidance regarding the issues that are most important for the author(s) to address. We discuss how to approach the revision process later in this chapter.

As mentioned in Chapter 1, it is rare that a manuscript is accepted after the initial review. Occasionally, the reviews are so positive and the proposed revisions so minor that an editor will decide to "conditionally accept" a paper. In such a case, there will not be much work for the author to do. Even so, follow the editor's guidance closely.

Usually, a positive outcome to the review process means that the author is invited to make revisions and then resubmit the paper. If the revisions are quite minor, the editor may decide to make a decision "in-house." In this case, the manuscript is not sent out for review a second time. However, the most common scenario is that a revised paper will be returned to the reviewers, who will reread and judge whether they like the revised paper sufficiently to now recommend acceptance. Depending on the journal and the editor, if the paper has been improved but the reviewers are not fully satisfied, the author may be asked to make further revisions. In other words, the paper then enters into a second cycle of revisions and may be reviewed a third time – or the editor may make the final decision in-house.

Editors usually will not go beyond a second round of revisions, but there are exceptions. In any case, as an author, evaluate whether the process is headed to an eventual acceptance. If so, each subsequent round of revisions should recognize the improvements to the paper, and ask for fewer and less cumbersome additional work. In other words, there should be fewer things to address in each subsequent round of revisions.

Most journals will return revised manuscripts to the same reviewers that evaluated the original version. Editors do not usually make a solid promise to *only* go back to these reviewers and occasionally bring in a new reviewer. Most often, this happens because one of the original reviewers is not available or declines to review the revision. In that case, editors have little choice but to find an alternative reviewer to obtain a complete set of reviews on the revised paper. For authors, it is usually beneficial that the paper is returned to the same reviewers. Since they have seen the previous version, they can attest that the author has done what was asked. A new reviewer could do this as well, especially since such a reviewer is usually given access to the original version, the decision letter, and the author's statement of revisions (more about that later in the chapter). However, a new reviewer also offers a fresh perspective and their comments may introduce new issues to be addressed. This can be frustrating for authors, but also puts the editor in a difficult spot: she cannot ignore the new reviewer's insights, but will also desire to move the process to a conclusion – rather than continuing a repeated cycle of evaluation and revision. The editor's judgment often depends on whether the additional comments can be accommodated easily and will markedly improve the paper. If so, the author will be asked to make the additional revisions.

Editors will usually strive to make a definitive decision on the manu-script after the revised paper has been evaluated. If the author is asked to complete a second round of revisions, there is a good chance that those will be evaluated in-house – especially if the additional revisions are quite minor. However, it is not inconceivable that a paper is rejected as this stage if the reviewers report – and the editor concurs – that the authors have not adequately engaged with the feedback and have not sufficiently improved the manuscript. We discuss strategies for avoiding this situation later in this chapter.

Finally, at journals that are edited by a team of multiple editors, the decision process may vary somewhat from the process we have just described. Depending on the decision model the editors have collectively agreed upon, they may have authorized one another to make decisions on the manuscripts assigned to each of them independently, or they may review some (or all) of the decisions collectively. Journals that receive very large numbers of manuscripts may seek a hybrid decision model. For instance, members of the editorial team may reject papers individually, but collectively decide to award opportunities to revise and resubmit, as well as acceptances of manuscripts. In the latter case, an editor will share the draft decision letter with the other editors and will advocate for the manuscript when the editors meet. The editor may explain to the other members of the editorial team why a specific manuscript deserves to move forward, why he thinks the revisions are doable, and what the paper will contribute to the field. The other team members will be able to look at the manuscript and the reviews in addition to having access to the draft decision letter. They will discuss the paper. If the team members agree, then the editor will send the decision letter to the submitting author. Many variations of this type of collective decision process are possible.

In sum, authors do not always receive a decision letter as soon as the required reviews have been submitted. Editor(s) need a little time to weigh the information they now have – and possibly consult with their editorial team members – to make a careful judgment about the manuscript.

2.4   BRUTAL REVIEWS – MOVING ON AFTER REJECTION

No matter how nicely worded, it is disappointing to receive notification that your manuscript has been "declined" – the euphemism editors often use to communicate a rejection. However, all scholars who submit their work to academic journals experience this – a lot. Consider that the most prestigious journals in political science and international relations have acceptance rates of 5 percent or less (of all submitted manuscripts). Of course, there are journals that offer better odds with acceptance rates of around 50 percent, but even such journals send out a lot of rejection letters. Here, we provide some context and then offer some strategies to overcome the many obstacles in the publishing process.

Of course, the acceptance rate is not exactly the same as the proportion of papers that receive invitations to revise and resubmit. The authors of accepted papers will have gone through the process of making revisions and a second (and maybe even third) round of review. Journals will occasionally reject a revised-and-resubmitted manuscript at a later stage. It is rare that an author does not resubmit a paper that received an invitation to revise and resubmit. In other words, the acceptance rate is not exactly the same as the proportion of papers that receive invitations to revise and resubmit. However, the difference tends to be small.

What is more important: these numbers convey that rejection is a very common experience for scholars. Whether scholars are inclined to send their work to journals with an acceptance rate of 5 or 50 percent, chances are that they have received a far larger number of rejection letters than acceptances over the course of their career. Weeks (2006: 879) points out that in baseball, "someone who gets a hit one-third of the time (thus failing to do so two-thirds of the time) is a huge success." Publishing in academic journals is not very different.

Although experience with, and knowledge of, the publication process is helpful, even the most successful scholars receive many rejection letters. Very few discuss this openly (Weeks 2006; Guardian Staff 2016). As a result, successes are highly visible on CVs, whereas "failures" largely remain hidden in private correspondence. The good news is that rejection at one journal does not mean the manuscript is doomed. Persistence pays. Move on to another journal and assume that every manuscript you produce will find a home eventually.

Decision letters for rejections are often quite brief. Editors do not always provide much information. On occasion, they will summarize the key reasons for the disappointing outcome of the review process. In doing so, editors usually point to the reviews. If you are lucky, either the editor or one of the reviewers suggests alternative outlets for your manuscript. This can be useful information, indicating that the manuscript may be a better fit for a different type of journal. It does not mean that you must send the paper there, but it provides insight into how one or more other scholars perceive the paper's contribution.

The decision letter is usually accompanied by two or more reviews. Even if professionally presented, the criticism can be difficult to read at first. Many scholars initially perceive the reviews as brutal. Rereading them some days later will provide a different perspective. Most often, once the initial impact of the rejection wears off, it is easier to appreciate the constructive value of the reviews. While some reviews are indeed brutal and unnecessarily harsh in tone, most reviewers will try to find something positive to say about the manuscript.

Quite often, what you receive is something akin to a "sandwich." The reviewer will say something positive about the paper, such as noting that the research question is interesting or novel. Next, he or she will discuss several shortcomings of the paper. Maybe the reviewer would have liked to see the paper's theoretical framing developed further, considers a different measure or statistical technique more appropriate, would have liked the case study to draw on more (or different) sources, questions your interpretation on a specific point, and so on. After the reviewer is done explaining all the shortcomings and possibly offering some suggestions as to how these might be rectified, the review will then end with something positive – sometimes a reiteration of the positive statement that opened the review.

Not all reviewers write this way. Some dive straight into a recitation of everything they dislike about your paper. Those reviews are more difficult to absorb on first reading – no one wants to feel like a failure. However, the review sandwiches can also lead to misinterpretation: some authors will wonder why the editor did not offer the opportunity to revise and resubmit after reading the introduction and conclusion of the review, and interpreting the middle from that positive vantage point. Rereading the middle more carefully after a day or so, it is easier to spot that the reviewer was less positive than it may have appeared at first glance.

Letting the reviews sit for a few days and rereading them after you have come to terms with the rejection is generally a good idea. After a little time has passed, it is easier to take a more dispassionate view. After considering the criticisms and the changes that the reviewers recommend, think carefully about the kinds of changes that will give the manuscript a better chance at the next journal.

Although you are not required to make revisions – after all, the manuscript gets to make a fresh start at a different journal – it is wise to do so. When revising for submission to a different journal, you have greater leeway in deciding what revisions to make than when you respond to an editor's invitation to revise and resubmit. In the latter case, you must carefully consider all recommendations. When you get a fresh start at a different journal, you will want to give careful thought to the revisions that will make the paper more likely to be reviewed positively at the next journal. Look for common themes between the reviews. If they all indicate that the theoretical framing of the paper could be strengthened, make sure to address that. If the reviewers ask for something that you know cannot be done, do not give up. Instead, explain in the text (or a footnote) why it cannot be done and why you chose the alternative approach you used. If you are unsure, discuss your strategy for what to revise on a rejected paper with a trusted colleague and/or mentor. Such a scholar need not be at the same institution. The person should be sufficiently knowledgeable about your area of research, as well as the specific constraints you face. Advice may differ depending on how urgently you need to have a publication to meet a deadline for a promotion or if you face expectations to publish in specific types of outlets.

To reiterate, carefully evaluate what revisions will help to make the paper more competitive. Seek to profit from the reviews to improve your work (Weeks 2006). That said, it is quite acceptable to leave some suggestions to the side. The goal in this situation is not to do everything the reviewers asked, but to give the paper a better chance at an invitation to revise and resubmit at the next journal. Besides, different reviewers are sure to ask for different modifications to the manuscript. Again, the goal is to improve the paper and give it a better chance at the next journal.

There is a second reason to make revisions before sending out a rejected manuscript to another journal. The manuscript may land on the desk of one of the same reviewers that read it previously. This does not always happen. The editor at the next journal will not know that the paper was rejected elsewhere and also will not know who may have reviewed it previously. The chance that the same reviewer is selected depends on the overall pool of scholars who can reasonably be asked to review the paper, which varies between research agendas, but it is always larger than zero.

In the discussion of the confidential comments that reviewers some-times share with editors, we indicated that they may reveal there that they saw the paper before. The reviewer may also include an evaluative statement there that the author will never see. This may be positive if the reviewer notes that the author used the comments from a previous review at another journal to improve the paper – even if he or she judges the changes to fall short of what should have been done – or negative if you ignored all suggestions and sent the paper straight to the next journal without changing anything at all.

What if you read the reviews and believe the reviewers – and possibly the editor, too – are wrong, incompetent or acting as gatekeepers? Do *not* pop off an email to the editor within the first 30 minutes after you receive the rejection. Put the reviews to the side and revisit them in a day or so. If, after some reflection and careful rereading of the reviews, you remain convinced that the review process was deeply flawed, carefully weigh your options. Realize that only a tiny portion of complaints about (perceived) problems with the review process are successful and rarely change the outcome in the author's favor (Simon et al. 1986). You could write to the editor to explain why and in what way the reviewers demonstrated their incompetence or why you think that the editor acted in a biased or arbitrary manner. It will take time and effort to do this – and even then, it may not make any difference. In essence, it may not be worth your time, even if you have a good argument. It may be better to focus on revisions and to quickly submit the paper elsewhere.

If you feel very strongly about incompetence or gatekeeping in the review process, you have a second option. It is possible to write an infor-mational letter to the editor. In this case, you start by explaining that you do not expect that the editor will change her mind, but that you want to explain why a specific reviewer was problematic. Present clear evidence that the reviewer is incompetent or is intent on gatekeeping. Although the presence of gatekeepers is often overstated, there is an occasional reviewer who does seek to prevent work in a specific area of inquiry from appearing in academic journals. If you believe you have evidence of this, you could present it to the editor for informational purposes. Editors are not experts on everything. If they are unaware of unresolved animosities between researchers with contrasting approaches to a subject, they may not be able to identify an effort to gatekeep. This kind of communication will not change the outcome of the review process and the manuscript can move on to the next journal without delay. The editor may find the information you provide useful or may put it to one side. In most cases, this will not be worth your time but on rare occasions, where something in the review process seems especially egregious, it is an option.

In sum, complaining to journal editors is not usually a productive use of time. That said, it is an option if something seems truly amiss. If you contemplate complaining, be sure to get a "second opinion" from a trusted and level-headed colleague.

2.5   REVISING FOR RESUBMISSION

It is wonderful to receive a much-coveted invitation to revise and resubmit – until you read the reviews. Then it sinks in that this is, in fact, an invitation to invest more hours of work into the paper. However, this time you will have some idea of what is needed to move the paper forward through your research pipeline. The amount of work to be done can vary substantially. Start by going through the reviews and note what changes the reviewers want you to make and then determine in what order you will tackle them.

Just as with a rejection, it is fine to set the reviews aside for a few days if the inventory of the requested revisions seems overwhelming at first. However, do not wait too long. A paper that received an invitation to revise and resubmit should become the highest priority on your "to do" list. Such an invitation does not guarantee that the revised paper will be accepted. Nevertheless, the odds of getting published are a lot better for carefully revised papers than for initial submissions. This time, you have a lot more information to help you turn the manuscript into a published article.

The editor's letter usually highlights the key issues that she would like you to address. Most often, the letter will end with the point that you should also pay attention to everything else the reviewers suggest. And you should. But paying careful attention to all the reviewers' comments is not the same as slavishly implementing every suggestion. In some cases, it may not be possible to follow every bit of advice, but you can acknowledge the value of all suggestions and respond to them.

Hence, our advice is slightly different from Lebo's (2016: 261), who suggested that authors "must diligently follow all of the reviewers' requests – you do not want to fall into that narrow category of papers rejected after an R&R." To give your manuscript the best possible chance of being accepted after revisions, it is important to demonstrate that you have taken all of the reviewers' suggestions seriously. This can be demonstrated most explicitly in the "statement of revisions," discussed in the next section, which is a written response that explains what you have done in response to the requests made by the editor and reviewers.

In devising your plan for revisions, keep a record. Have notes of your plan and keep careful track of all the changes you make to the manuscript. This will help later, when you are ready to draft the statement of revisions.

First, pay attention to the editor's letter. Most often, the editor will indicate the key issues that must be addressed. Whether or not she explicitly references the reviews in doing so, these issues are usually also the key themes in the reviews. Make sure to note this, because it means that in accommodating the editor's requests, you are simultaneously addressing some of the reviewers' suggestions.

Second, comb carefully through each of the reviews and determine how you will respond to the remaining reviewer suggestions. Some requests may be straightforward and easy to accommodate, such as a request to include an additional reference on some point. Even if you think it does not add anything of significance, including it is the most pragmatic solution. A reviewer may also ask for a clarification or the inclusion of a caveat. In the former case, add or expand on a definition. In the latter case, an explanatory note usually is sufficient.

Other requests may be more difficult or quite time-consuming to address. In other cases, the author may disagree with the reviewer, or two reviewers point in opposite directions. The last situation often causes scholars the greatest agony, especially if they have received advice similar to that dispensed by Lebo (2016). While that advice is well-intended, the paper would lose focus if two contradictory pieces of advice are both accommodated. In this situation, make sure to carefully consider the merits of both suggestions. Decide which, in your view, is the better fit for the paper's core research question and keep notes on your reasoning in support of accommodating one reviewer over the other. Chances are that the reviewer whose recommendation you did not implement will appreciate being taken seriously and will accept your explanation. And if he does not, the editor will very likely realize that you had to choose one option and appreciate that you carefully weighed the two proposed strategies.

Follow a similar process when you disagree with a reviewer's recommendation. This is a bit more risky, because the reviewer may dig in his heels and insist that you make the desired change and recommend that the paper should be rejected if you do not. Whether this risk is worth taking depends on the situation. Ultimately, the manuscript is your work and, if accepted, will be published with your name on it. If following the reviewer's suggestion would result in an article you would be embarrassed to claim as yours, do not make the revision. However, carefully pick your battles. In most cases, you can revise the paper in such a way as to accommodate the reviewer while also maintaining the integrity of your own intellectual identity. Once again, this is the kind of situation where it makes sense to obtain feedback from a trusted colleague and/or mentor, who can help you take a step back and think logically about the best course of action.

In yet other situations it may be undesirable or impossible to accommodate a reviewer request. This can usually be explained. For instance, a reviewer may suggest that you use a different measure and state that "surely there must be data on ..." You may have already looked for that specific type of data and know that it does not exist, or only for a very small sample or for a very limited number of years. In this case, you cannot accommodate the request, but you can explain why – and should do so in the statement of revisions. It is useful to be specific and explain what sources do exist, what their limitations are, why you elected not to use them, and why the measure you used instead is adequate.

The same holds for situations in which a reviewer suggests that you use a statistical technique that, to your best knowledge, is not appropriate. Rather than revising the paper to use the recommended method, explain why you are using the technique you chose and why it is appropriate. In this case, it is useful if you can cite articles from methodologists who recommend the technique you use. This may persuade the reviewer and will show the editor that you have carefully considered your choice of statistical technique.

Finally, never forego making a recommended revision simply because it is difficult to do or would be time-consuming. If the reviewers suggest that the case studies need to go beyond the use of secondary sources, then find original material to use. Even if there are limitations in what you can access, you can probably expand the range of sources to make the case studies richer and more persuasive. If a reviewer suggests you add a control variable and rerun your analyses, it is best to follow the advice. Depending on the size of the dataset and the number of analyses you completed, this can be a lot of work. However, it will be important to show that this additional variable does not significantly alter your original results.

Do not confuse the nature of the revision – major or minor – with the amount of work involved. In general, a major revision will indeed be more work that a minor one. But it is possible for a minor revision to take a lot of hours to complete. If so, the revisions may not alter the fundamental argument of the paper, but may simply be tedious and time-consuming. Whichever it is, revisions are always worth the effort: chances are quite good that you will end with the conviction that the manuscript has substantially benefitted from the changes by the time you are ready to return it to the editor.

In sum, tackle recommended revisions seriously and thoughtfully. Although there are situations in which you may have good reason to not meticulously implement all requests, make sure that you have solid arguments with which to defend your choices. Note that we recommend to always carefully consider your options and, preferably, consult with a colleague and/or mentor you trust. In addition, provide a logically coherent explanation for your choices in the statement of revisions. Seek to be responsive to the reviewers, but use your judgment.

2.6   WRITING A "STATEMENT OF REVISIONS"

After completing the revisions, it is time to write an explanation of what you did in response to the editor's and reviewers' requests. This explanation is called the statement of revisions. Journals typically require that such a statement accompany a revised manuscript. While it can be a bit tedious to put together, it is also very important to take the time to do it well.

This statement is your opportunity to explain and defend what you have done in response to the reviewers' comments. It is also your opportunity to demonstrate that you have taken the revision process seriously. Both the editor and the reviewers will appreciate a well-organized statement of revisions with clear explanations of what you changed – and what you did not.

First, check the editor's letter inviting you to revise and resubmit for any restrictions on the length of the statement of revisions. Very often, there will not be any such restrictions, but occasionally an editor sets limits on the length of this statement. If there is such a restriction, be sure to adhere to it.

Second, you will need to choose how to organize the statement of revisions. To ensure that you respond to every comment made by the editor and the reviewers, copy the letter and reviews into a separate file. Delete the salutation and introductory material on the letter and keep only the paragraph(s) in which the editor describes the key issues she wants you to address. Above the paragraphs, add in capital letters: "editor's comments." Below the paragraph, add in capital letters: "response." Below this, explain the changes made in response to the editor's request(s). Follow this same pattern with the reviews. Add the heading, in capital letters: "reviewer 1, comment 1" and follow it with your response. Keep going in this fashion until you have responded to each comment from each reviewer. If there is overlap between the reviewers' requests, you do not need to repeat the exact same explanation. Instead, indicate as a response something like: "see my response to comment 3 by reviewer 1." The reason to use capital letters for the headings is that many online submission systems ask you to paste the statement of revisions into a box that does not preserve most other formatting, such as using bold for the headings. Of course, if you upload the statement of revisions as a separate document, you can use whichever formatting helps the editor and reviewers to easily spot that you have addressed all of their concerns.

A statement of revisions structured along these lines is easy to write and ensures that all comments have been addressed, but it may get very repetitive – or contain lots of references to earlier responses. Hence, if there is a lot of overlap between the comments of the editor and reviewers, it makes sense to organize the statement of revisions by request. In this case, you write a brief statement that summarizes the request, such as: "the editor and reviewers 1 and 3 all asked for the case studies to be enhanced with original source materials." Then explain what you have done in response. Next, do the same for the remaining requests. Place the requests highlighted by the editor at the top, followed by the requests made by multiple reviewers, and concluding with the requests made by only one reviewer.

There is no need to use the same format for every statement of revisions you write. Use the format that communicates most efficiently in a given situation. If there is little or no overlap between the requests from the various reviewers, then it makes sense to structure the statement by reviewer. This will make sure that the reviewers can easily see that you have carefully attended to each of their specific comments.

However, if the reviewers all address the same issues, the repetitive nature of this structure becomes very tedious to read. Therefore, in such a situation it is better to group the responses by request. Outlines of these two ways of organizing the statement of revisions are shown in Box 2.1. We do not claim that these are the only ways to organize such a statement, but emphasize that you want to make it as easy as possible for the editor and reviewers to spot what you have done in response to their requests.

In addition to these substantive issues, it is customary to preface the statement of revisions with a brief note of thanks to the editor – for the opportunity to revise – and to the reviewers – for the usefulness of the comments. At the end of the review, acknowledge that the comments have led to an improved manuscript and express the hope that the revisions you have made are satisfactory to the editor and reviewers. Do not sign the statement with your name, although it is fine to sign off with "sincerely, the author."

BOX 2.1 TWO WAYS TO ORGANIZE THE STATEMENT OF REVISIONS

By Reviewer	By Request
EDITOR'S COMMENTS ... RESPONSE ...	The Editor, Reviewer 1, and Reviewer 3 all suggested that ... In response, I/we have made the following changes ...
REVIEWER 1, COMMENT 1 ... RESPONSE ...	Reviewers 1 and 2 both suggested ... In response, ...
REVIEWER 1, COMMENT 2 ... RESPONSE ...	Reviewers 2 and 3 suggested ... In response ... Reviewer 1 suggested ... In response ...
REVIEWER 2, COMMENT 1 ... RESPONSE ...	Reviewer 2 commented that ... In response ... Reviewer 3 suggested ... In response ...
REVIEWER 3, COMMENT 1 ...	

2.7   ACCEPTED! BUT NOT DONE YET – THE FINAL MS AND COPY-EDITING STAGE

After putting lots of work into a manuscript and revising it several times, a letter that announces that the article has been accepted for publication is a thrill. Enjoy that wonderful feeling. Then read the "small print" that follows the good news. After acceptance of the paper, there will still be several steps to complete before the article is officially in print.

A number of journals that publish quantitative articles in political science and international relations now seek to verify the statistical analyses presented in manuscripts. Information about such a policy is included in the author's guidelines, so anyone who submits their work to such a journal will know this upfront. Journals with replication policies often do not accept a manuscript outright. Instead, they add the caveat that the acceptance is conditional on their ability to replicate the paper's statistical analyses. The author is asked to provide the journal's editors with the dataset and the code used to complete the analyses. Once everything checks out, the manuscript is fully accepted and moved forward into production – which includes a series of steps between the manuscript's acceptance and appearance of the article in print. Manuscripts that contain theoretical contributions or case studies are not usually subjected to this type of verification. We discuss this in more detail in Chapter 4.

After acceptance, the editorial office usually asks for a final version of the manuscript. This version will include the author's name and institutional affiliation – there is now no longer any reason for the paper to be anonymized. If there are references you excluded to preserve the double-blind nature of the review process, these can now be added in. For instance, if you wish to include a reference to your dissertation or add additional self-citations, now is the time to add these. Be sure that you include both an in-text citation and an entry in the reference list. If the item appears in only one or the other, the copy editor will ask questions. If the journal accommodates an author's note, you can now include a note thanking people who provided feedback on early drafts of the paper. If the paper is co-authored, you can now add the note explaining the contributions each made to the final product, as explained in Chapter 1 (see also Box 1.2).

This is also a good time to check the manuscript for any remaining typos and to make sure that all works cited in the text are included in the reference list, and that the citations are complete, accurate, and in the format required by the journal. Conversely, make sure that there are no extra entries in the reference list, such as works you cited in a previous version that are no longer referenced in the text. For in-text citations that list multiple works within parentheses, check whether the journal style is to list these in chronological, reverse chronological, or alphabetical order. Make sure the list uses the correct order.

Although almost all journal publishers will have a copy editor review the typeset manuscript, waiting for these professionals to catch your mistakes is not always a great idea. The copy editor usually returns the "page proofs" to the author, with the request to approve changes and provide missing information within a short window of time. Page proofs are the typeset version of the article. The pages will look as they will appear in the journal. The page proofs are accompanied by a set of "queries," or questions, that you will be asked to resolve quickly – sometimes as little as 48 hours. Consider that you may receive this request when you are traveling and not able to quickly retrieve the necessary information about an article's correct publication year or a chapter's pages in an edited volume. Such a situation is best avoided. With a bit of time and attention to detail before you turn in the final manuscript to the editorial office, you can save yourself having to scramble for requested information at an inconvenient time. You may not achieve zero queries, but you want to minimize the number of issues you have to resolve.

Journals vary in how they handle situations in which an author fails to respond within the given time window. Sometimes the article goes forward and is printed with awkward mistakes still present. Other journals will simply delay publication. Neither situation is desirable. Again, a bit of attention when finalizing the accepted manuscript can help you avoid problems later.

After completing the post-acceptance steps – the replication check, final manuscript, copy-editing, and page proofs – it is once again time to wait. Increasingly, journals publish the finalized article online ahead of it being assigned to a specific volume and issue. In Chapter 1, we mentioned that journals often have section of their webpage listing the newest articles as "first view" or "early view." Such articles are considered to be published and are fully accessible to the journal's subscribers. Most likely, you will receive a PDF of the article at this point.

The only additional step will be assignment to a volume and issue. This changes the page numbers (which always start at 1 for online publication) and, possibly, the year of publication. For instance, the article may have first appeared online in 2019 and is assigned to a specific issue in 2020.

The copyright will be given as 2019, but the volume and issue number will be dated 2020. The pagination will be adjusted to reflect the article's place in the sequence of all articles published in the issues of the relevant volume. In each volume, only the first article in the first issue will start on page 1.

After publication, focus not only on publishing additional articles, but also try to maximize the impact of the work that is now in print. In Chapter 6 we discuss in more detail what you can do to get your work noticed – and cited.

NOTE

1. These desk reject rates are based on the annual reports of the various journals mentioned.

3.   Ethics and integrity in publishing

There is growing interest in promoting research and publication ethics in political science and international relations. Desposato (2016a) links this to the increased use of experimental methods in a discipline that has long been focused on observational studies and surveys. He notes that experiments conducted in international settings – and especially in the global South – are highly likely to create ethical dilemmas, but recognizes that the problem is present in experimental research in the USA and Europe as well (Desposato 2016a: 3).

This growing importance of research and publication ethics is in part driven by the increased use of experimental methods, but also comes on the heels of discoveries of fabrication and other questionable research practices (Willis 2014; Singal 2015; Van Noorden 2015; Desposato 2016a). These events underscore the importance of ethics and integrity in publishing.

Although discussions about this subject often quickly converge on the topic of experiments and field research, ethics and integrity matter in almost every aspect of research and publishing. To recognize the broader importance of this subject matter in the discipline, this chapter reviews a number of issues regarding ethics and integrity. The focus is on issues that are closely related to writing and publishing journal articles, but because these activities are closely intertwined with the research process we cannot avoid a broader discussion of research ethics. After all, journal articles usually report on research.

3.1   RESEARCH AND PUBLICATION ETHICS

Research and publication ethics encompass a complex terrain. This chapter sketches key aspects and maps out responsible and questionable practices, as well as misconduct. What makes research and publication ethics so complex is that, although some practices constitute clear cases of misconduct, there are many others that may be acceptable in some circumstances but suspect in others. We address some of the more straightforward issues before introducing the less well-defined ones.

The most serious forms of research misconduct are fabrication, falsification and plagiarism (FFP). The Office of Research Integrity (ORI) in
the US Department of Health and Human Services provides definitions
of each of the three concepts and associated behaviors, which are widely
understood to be unacceptable (Martinson et al. 2005; Jordan and Hill
2012; Roig 2015; Van Noorden 2015; WCRIF 2020).

First, fabrication is defined as "making up data or results and record-
ing or reporting them" (ORI n.d.). Second, falsification is described as
"manipulating research materials, equipment, or processes, or changing
or omitting data or results such that the research is not accurately represented in the research record" (ORI n.d.). Note that both definitions
reference not only the research process, but also allude to the reporting of
research in publications. Third, plagiarism is defined as "the appropriation of another person's ideas, processes, results, or words without giving
appropriate credit" (ORI n.d.). We address plagiarism in more depth in
the next section. Here, we focus on fabrication and falsification as well as
some other examples of problematic practices.

Before delving further into these issues, however, we explore briefly
why ethics and integrity are vital for scholarship. Misconduct in research
and publication damages not only the reputation of the scholar(s) who
engage(s) in this behavior; it also damages the reputation of scholarship
more generally, and risks reducing public support for and trust in science
and scholarship (Martinson et al. 2005).

Research integrity depends on standards for responsible research
practices that set out expectations for honesty and accuracy in planning,
conducting and reporting research (Moher et al. 2020; WCRIF 2020).
Traditionally, most scholars learnt about acceptable practices from their
advisors in graduate school. Increasingly, professional societies offer
opportunities to learn about professional standards and responsible practices as well. Most of these are not unique to a specific discipline, but are
broadly shared understandings of responsible and ethical scholarship.
The goal is to ensure that both scholars and the broader public are able to
trust that published scholarship meets standards of validity and trustworthiness (Moher et al. 2020; WCRIF 2020).

Of course, the importance of ethical conduct does not guarantee
universal adherence to it. Moreover, Moher et al. (2020: 3) note that conventional measures by which scholars are evaluated and rewarded – such
as the number of publications and citations – reveal very little about "the
rigor of their work." In fact, they worry that the pressure to publish oper-

ates as a disincentive to maintain responsible research practices (Moher et al. 2020; see also Martinson et al. 2005; Jordan and Hill 2012).

Deviation from responsible research practices can take a variety of forms. Among these, the intentional fabrication or falsification of data or other research materials represents the "most serious threat to the scientific enterprise" (Roig 2015: 2). In other words, making up data is unacceptable, as is manipulating, changing or omitting data. Doing so fundamentally distorts the scientific record: it presents fraudulent conclusions that are based on false facts. Unfortunately, it can be difficult to discover this type of deception.

Consider, for instance, the case of an article written by two political scientists and published in the journal *Science*. The article appeared in December 2014. It was subsequently discovered to be based on fabricated data and was retracted in May 2015 (Carey 2015; Gelman 2015). The article had been a collaboration between Michael LaCour, then a graduate student affiliated with the University of California Los Angeles (UCLA), and Donald Green, a professor at Columbia University. The latter said that he had "taken his collaborator's data on faith" (Gelman 2015). This suggests that both LaCour's co-author and the journal *Science* trusted that the data had been genuine and had been collected according to the protocol described in the study. Such trust is not unusual.

The deception was discovered by David Broockman, who was then a graduate student at the University of California, Berkeley (UC Berkeley). He wanted to conduct a similar study and became troubled by various oddities in the data (Carey 2015; Singal 2015; Van Noorden 2015). With the help of fellow graduate student, Joshua Kalla, and Yale University political scientist Peter Aronow, Broockman eventually was able to demonstrate that the LaCour study was based on "brazen data fraud" (Singal 2015). The three scholars showed that LaCour had taken an existing survey, which he treated as the first wave of a panel study, and then added additional waves by fabricating responses to subsequent questionnaires administered to the same group of respondents (Singal 2015). The study he claimed to have done had in fact never occurred.

Although less than half a year elapsed between the study's publication in *Science* and its retraction at the request of Green, Broockman had known about the study for much longer (Carey 2015; Gelman 2015; Singal 2015). His efforts to make sense of unusual patterns in the data predated the study's publication (Singal 2015). They were slowed down in part because other scholars discouraged Broockman from exposing the fraudulent work that had been co-authored by a rising star and a well-established scholar (Singal 2015). This, too, is not at all unusual.

This case exposed the weak protocols in place in political science and international relations to discover data fabrication, as well as the willingness of scholars to trust one another and, especially, to trust those affiliated with prestigious institutions. However, in response to this and other scandals, the discipline has begun to address these issues. First, it has become much more common for journals to verify that scholars obtained approval for human subjects research reported in their manuscripts. Approval for such research by an Institutional Review Board (IRB) is standard protocol for human subjects research at universities in the USA and many other countries – something we discuss in a later section of this chapter. *Science* did not check whether LaCour had obtained such approval from his university and there is no evidence that he ever did (Van Noorden 2015). Had the absence of such approval been discovered earlier, it might have led to further questions about the data. That, in turn, might have brought LaCour's deception to light sooner.

Second, in recent years many journals have added the requirement that authors provide the data and the code used to obtain the results reported in a manuscript. Such journals communicate to authors that they will publish a manuscript only if the analyses can be replicated by the publication's chosen replication specialist. This step usually takes place after a paper has been accepted, i.e., after the review process has been completed. In addition, many journals now demand that authors make the data and code available to other researchers either through the publisher's website or another reliable data repository. *Science* did not ask LaCour for the data, did not attempt a replication of his analysis, and did not require him to make his data accessible to other researchers. We discuss the issue of data access and research transparency in Chapter 4. We note here that it is unlikely that simply replicating the analysis with the code provided by the author would have revealed that the data was fabricated. Hence, this step, while valuable, is not designed to detect fabrication and falsification. Instead, this type of replication ensures that the analysis is reported accurately and guards against detrimental research practices, as defined by the WCRIF (2020).

Third, as Broockman observes, there are structural impediments to exposing fabrication and falsification in the discipline (cited in Singal 2015). He was repeatedly dissuaded from exposing the problems he suspected to be present in the LaCour data and notes that there are no clear protocols for bringing fraud to the attention of the discipline (Singal 2015; see also Van Noorden 2015).

The LaCour case received a lot of publicity and shocked political scientists, but it is neither unique nor the most egregious in the social sciences. A few years before the LaCour case broke, it came to light that a Dutch psychologist, Diederik Stapel, had fabricated experimental results for years. His repeated data fabrication affected at least 55 journal articles, as well as the PhD dissertations of ten of his students (Bhattacharjee 2013).

It is difficult to know precisely how often this type of gross misconduct happens. A survey by Martinson et al. (2005) did not ask explicitly about data fabrication, but did ask about falsification. Less than a half percent of respondents admitted to having falsified research data, but slightly more than 15 percent agreed that they had dropped observations or data points "based on a gut feeling that they were inaccurate" (Martinson et al. 2005: 737). This gut feeling led researchers to "massage" the data to better conform to their expectations. As indicated by the definition provided above, this behavior is a form of data falsification (ORI n.d.). The difference between the responses to the two items underscores that self-reports of behavior are "likely to lead to under-reporting and therefore to conservative estimates," an issue of which the authors were aware (Martinson et al. 2005: 738; see also Tijdink et al. 2014).

The frequency of data fabrication is impossible to ascertain – we only know of those cases where the misconduct was eventually discovered. While it is a serious problem that distorts the scientific record (Roig 2015), Bhattacharjee (2013) suggests that it "might represent a lesser threat to the integrity of science than the massaging of data and selective reporting of experiments." The WCRIF (2020) echoes this sentiment. Unfortunately, these forms of falsification and other questionable research practices are not any easier to detect than fabrication.

Although journals have become more proactive in requiring ethical assurances from scholars who submit their work, Wilson et al. (2016) note that the ability of editors to evaluate adherence to ethical standards is limited. That said, Jordan and Hill (2012) found that more journals required a data sharing plan than required evidence that approval for human subjects research (through an IRB or equivalent) had been obtained. However, they also noted that, overall, "few journals in political science require assurance statements" (Jordan and Hill 2012: 243). This has already begun to change. Journals increasingly require not only a data sharing plan, but are also more likely to check the analyses presented in accepted articles.

Data sharing is discussed in more detailed in Chapter 4. Providing data access to other researchers is part of responsible research practices, but differs from research ethics. The accessibility of data may make it easier to uncover certain types of ethical transgressions (such as data fabrication), but would not readily reveal other questionable practices.

3.2   PLAGIARISM

Almost all scholars have heard of plagiarism, as warnings against it are quite prevalent in higher education. Hence, by the time you begin to produce publishable manuscripts, this concept may seem quite familiar. As a student, you may have been told that copying from existing scholarship is unacceptable. However, plagiarism goes beyond the literal copying of another scholar's work. It is important to achieve a more nuanced understanding of the various practices that may be considered plagiaristic; a deeper knowledge of the concept provides you with better tools to ensure adherence to ethical practices in writing and publishing.[1]

In the previous section, plagiarism was defined as "the appropriation of another person's ideas, processes, results, or words without giving appropriate credit" (ORI n.d.). This definition indicates that plagiarism is not limited to literal copying of text, although that is certainly one of its manifestations. In fact, it is probably the most easily detectable form of plagiarism, especially since the emergence of plagiarism detection software such as Turnitin (http://www.turnitin.com) or iThenticate (http://www.ithenticate.com). The former is used at many universities in the USA and the latter is increasingly employed by academic journals in political science and international relations. Such software produces a "similarity score," which editors can use to evaluate whether the text of a submitted manuscript is sufficiently original.

Despite the increased use of such tools to systematically screen all submitted manuscripts by well-established journals, plagiarism remains a problem of unknown proportions. The use of screening tools is not universal and it does not catch all forms of plagiarism. McGuire (2010: 111) suggests that "[p]lagiarism in political science probably exists to a greater degree than we realize." His own work was plagiarized. However, the author who stole McGuire's work had used an earlier version of the published article that he had made available on his website (McGuire 2010). The plagiarized article represented an earlier version of McGuire's article, which had been significantly revised after review and before it was published (McGuire 2010). The revisions could have made it more difficult for software to detect the misconduct (had the journal used it), because it lessened the similarities in the text of McGuire's published article and the plagiarized one.

Despite the difficulties in detecting plagiarism, the tally kept by the blog Retraction Watch (http://retractionwatch.com/) suggests that political science journals have retracted articles with some frequency in the past decade when they have been judged to have been plagiarized. Most – but not all – of the retracted articles were published in smaller, field-specific journals. This record suggests that there is now a greater willingness to take action when misconduct is identified, but also that smaller journals may be less able to invest in the personnel and tools to detect it.

To avoid being accused of plagiarizing text, make sure to take precise notes when consulting source materials, to always place literal quotes within quotation marks, and to place the source citation after the quote (Roig 2015). This way, you acknowledge the source and give "appropriate credit to its author" (Roig 2015: 6).

The same principle – providing appropriate credit to the original author – applies to other aspects of plagiarism as well. This is why it is unacceptable to "paraphrase" by taking another author's text, changing some of the words or simply substituting synonyms for key words, and passing it off as your own. Although this form of plagiarism is more difficult to detect, it is no less egregious. Further, this sort of "paraphrasing" does not conform to common understandings of what it means to characterize someone else's work in your own words.

Like quoting literal text from a source, paraphrasing also requires that the source of the material is credited, but instead of using the literal words of the original author in quotation marks, it involves restating the author's argument or information in your own words. As Roig (2015) notes, paraphrasing requires not only that you use your own words, but also your own sentence structure. In addition, the paraphrased material must faithfully represent the original author's meaning (Roig 2015).

There are some exceptions to these rules regarding quotation and paraphrasing that pertain to specialized or highly technical language. For instance, many political scientists use similar phrases when discussing the results of statistical tests, such as: "Hypothesis 1 shows that …" or "the results do not support Hypothesis 2." Readers would expect to find such stock phrases in an article reporting quantitative analysis. In addition, Roig (2015: 14) argues that "the limited use of identical or nearly-identical phrases which describe a commonly-used methodology" are permitted, largely because the use of such phrases would not be considered misleading.

A more difficult situation is the use of information that scholars might view as common knowledge, which does not need attribution. Roig (2015) suggests that what can be considered common knowledge is highly context dependent. What is commonly known among scholars in a specific discipline may be new information for those in another. In addition, scholarly communities in the same discipline that are separated geographically may not fully share the same base of common knowledge. For example, political scientists in the USA, irrespective of specialization, may regard certain facts about the US political system to be common knowledge. However, for a political scientist trained in Japan or Norway, those same facts are less likely to count as common knowledge and would require attribution. On the other hand, assuming they all use quantitative methods in their work, political scientists from the USA, Japan and Norway are likely to use the same stock phrases regarding hypothesis-testing when writing in English. In sum, as the discipline becomes increasingly international, scholars will need to be more careful in considering what information may be considered common knowledge and what requires a source citation.

Thus far, the discussion of plagiarism has focused on problems with failing to cite the work of other scholars. However, re-using text from your own earlier work – or text recycling – is also considered plagiarism; Roig (2015) notes that papers have been retracted for doing this. The blog Retraction Watch (http://retractionwatch.com/) provides evidence, listing several papers in political science that have been retracted in recent years because of what it terms duplication. Retraction Watch explicitly equates duplication with self-plagiarism and uses this term to indicate that either all or parts of an article have already appeared in print elsewhere and are "repeated … without appropriate citation" (Retraction Watch n.d.).

Hence, it is important to take seriously the problem of text recycling. Roig (2015) suggests that this form of plagiarism is more likely to occur when a scholar produces a series of related papers and re-uses portions of a literature review or other elements verbatim in several manuscripts. Although it might be tempting to do this if the arguments of two or more papers rely on the same body of literature, it should not be inordinately difficult to rewrite the literature review to tailor it to each piece and to cite your own related work where this is appropriate.

There is a legal aspect to the prohibition on text recycling. Once published, copyright attaches to the work and gives the publisher of the journal in which the article appears certain rights. This is explained in the copyright agreement you sign before the article appears in print. If (parts of) the same text appear in a subsequent article, they need to be attributed to the original author (yourself) by placing the material in quotation marks and adding a citation after the quote. If this is not done, you violate the rights that the publisher of your earlier work has acquired. You cannot legitimately sign copyright agreements for the same text with two separate publishers, even if it is "only" the literature review. By re-using text you risk retraction of the subsequent article.

Self-plagiarism is differentiated by the use of a scholar's own words that have already appeared in print elsewhere without attribution to the work in which those words originally appeared. Hence, the difference between plagiarism and self-plagiarism hinges on who authored the text that is being copied. Whether you plagiarize the work of someone else or yourself, if the misconduct is discovered the penalties may not be dramatically different.

All that said, the same exceptions regarding stock phrases and standard descriptions of methods and/or procedures apply to self-plagiarism as well. Further, copyright generally does not attach to conference papers, working papers, or papers posted in online paper archives. However, it is a good idea to check what rights you retain – and which ones you potentially lose – when you include your work in such repositories.

Although plagiarism is most easily addressed in the context of similarity between texts, as we have done thus far, it also applies to ideas, processes and results (ORI n.d.). In this context, it is important to understand also that plagiarism need not be conscious or intentional. It is possible to remember an idea but not where you first encountered it (Roig 2015). This can make it difficult to avoid unintentional misconduct. If, despite your best efforts to consistently acknowledge the contributions of others, you realize that you have unintentionally overlooked the source of an idea, do your best to rectify the oversight. For a work that has already been published, you can ask the editor and/or publisher to append a correction to the original published work to include the additional source.

However, it is also possible for plagiarism of ideas to be intentional. For instance, Roig (2015) notes that some scholars use the review process as a source for ideas or take credit for the ideas of their students. Neither of these actions represents ethical behavior and should be avoided.

In sum, the literal copying of text – whether authored by others or yourself – is the type of plagiarism that is most easily identified, but it is by no means the only form of it. Although more difficult to demonstrate persuasively, the plagiarism of ideas, processes and results also represents a serious form of research misconduct. These other forms create a more complicated picture of the various guises in which plagiarism can make an appearance in scholarly work.

3.3   ORIGINALITY AND "SALAMI SLICES"

The core problem of all forms of plagiarism is that the work is presented as an original effort by its author when it is not. Although not all forms of plagiarism are easy to adjudicate, addressing the practice of "salami slicing" is even more difficult. Salami slicing is named for a type of cured sausage that is eaten in thin slices. The thinner the slices, the more slices can be cut from the sausage. If a research project represents the entire sausage, salami slicing refers to cutting it up into the smallest possible segments to yield as many publications as possible. The project is divided into the "least publishable unit" (Roig 2015: 19).

The practice of squeezing as many articles as possible out of a research project has its source in two countervailing pressures: on the one hand is the pressure to publish, on the other the difficult and time-consuming process of gathering evidence and/or coding data. Although many scholars experience an intensified pressure to publish, they cannot easily expand the time and resources available to gather data. One solution to this dilemma is to get more out of the available data, i.e., to produce as many articles as possible on the basis of the data and information you already have in hand.

However, doing so can be risky. If the process of deriving a number of articles from one research project is pushed to an extreme, the value added of each piece becomes exceedingly small and there may be significant overlap between them. The latter problem is one that we discussed in the previous section of this chapter: the risk of duplication of text between the various articles that address related questions and are based on the same dataset. This problem can potentially be avoided by carefully crafting each piece to avoid re-using the same text. The problem of the scientific value of each article suggests that an effort to produce ever thinner salami slices has diminishing returns: as the number of articles derived from one project gets larger, each additional article will offer less novel content. Although it may be possible to publish a lot of small slices, it is extremely unlikely that you will be able to place them in very prestigious journals.

Avoiding salami slicing does not mean that you cannot derive multiple articles from one research project. It does mean that it is important to exercise judgment and to be transparent about the relationship of several manuscripts to one another and the research project from which they are derived. In some cases, segmenting a larger project into several articles may be "the most meaningful approach to reporting the results of that research" (Roig 2015: 19).

It is important to ask what each of several manuscripts that are based on a single research project offers. If the project offers enough material to produce several distinct manuscripts, then it is certainly acceptable to do so. For instance, PhD dissertation projects in political science and international relations are often planned to yield multiple article-length manuscripts that address a set of related questions. The dissertation may build on original research or a new dataset that is designed to facilitate the production of multiple articles. Such efforts are not considered salami slices. Nor does it necessarily need to be problematic to produce additional articles – beyond those planned as part of the dissertation project – from the data collected for the dissertation project. However, at some point, every scholar has to ask whether the next paper to be produced from the same project can be justified or whether it represents an effort to keep eating crumbs from a largely empty plate after the entire salami has already been consumed.

As with many aspects of ethics and integrity in publishing, the boundary between the justifiable production of multiple articles from a research project and going too far is not always easily ascertained. Some sources suggest that strategies like adding a new variable to the dataset or, conversely, dropping data (i.e., using part of the dataset) do not justify an additional publication (Roig 2015). Although such practices could be questionable, they could also be justified and lead to interesting additional insights. Again, what is acceptable is a judgment call. When seeking to produce additional articles from a research project – beyond those envisioned when the project was planned – ask yourself: What new insights does it yield? What is the scientific value of the additional paper? An honest answer to such questions will establish whether or not you should embark on writing the additional manuscript or whether you may be trying to slice the salami a bit too thin.

3.4   HUMAN SUBJECTS RESEARCH AND IRB APPROVAL

Ethical research practices are especially important when research involves human subjects – also called participants (Schwartz-Shea and Yanow 2016). The failure to adhere to high ethical standards can harm those subjects in a variety of ways. Among the most abhorrent examples are the medical experiments inflicted on concentration camp prisoners by German doctors and scientists during World War II. Their trial, after the war, led to the enumeration of essential principles for the conduct of experiments involving human subjects, known as the Nuremberg Code (The Belmont Report 1979; Desposato 2016b; Seligson 2016).

The first principle of the Nuremberg Code requires voluntary consent by the individual, which presumes both the legal capacity to give consent and the ability to choose freely – i.e., without coercion – *and* with sufficient knowledge of what the experiment will entail to be able to make an informed judgment (The Belmont Report 1979; United States Holocaust Memorial Museum 2020).

This first principle was violated not only by German doctors and scientists during World War II, but also by the United States Public Health Service's Tuskegee Study that was initiated in 1932 (Centers for Disease Control and Prevention (CDC) 2020). The study involved hundreds of Black men from a poor rural county in Alabama and sought to evaluate whether it might be better to forego the existing – but often dangerous – treatments for syphilis (Seligson 2016). The study went on for decades, even after penicillin proved to be a safe and effective treatment in 1947. The study's participants were never offered the option of quitting the study and receiving this treatment (Seligson 2016; CDC 2020). In fact, the study did not end until it was exposed by the press in 1972 (Seligson 2016; CDC 2020). A subsequent investigation established that, even though the study's participants had given their consent, they had been misled about its real purpose and had not been offered treatment (CDC 2020).

It is unethical to mislead participants, because it calls into question the value of their consent to participate in the study. It is also unethical to withhold a safe and effective treatment. To address the ethical problems that had been uncovered by the investigation of the Tuskegee study, the US Congress in 1974 passed the National Research Act. Subsequently, a panel of experts produced the Belmont Report (1979), which provided guidelines for the ethical conduct of research with human subjects (Seligson 2016; CDC 2020).

Misconduct regarding human subjects research is not limited to medical science. One of the best-known ethical lapses in the social sciences is represented by the experiments conducted in the 1960s by Stanley Milgram, a social psychologist who was at that time affiliated with Yale University (Nissani 1990; Seligson 2016). He sought to demonstrate that obedience to authority trumps judgment in an experiment in which the participants were asked to administer increasingly stronger electric shocks to another person. He showed that most participants continued to administer the shocks, even when those reached a level at which they could do serious harm, when encouraged by an authority figure (Nissani 1990; Seligson 2016).[2] These experiments were considered unethical, because they had the potential to traumatize the participants who administered the shocks. The ostensible recipients of the shocks were actors and not actually subjected to electric shocks, but the participants were not told this. In addition, subjects were told they were participating in a study of memory and learning – a misleading characterization that calls into question whether they were able to make an informed judgment about their participation in the study.

These examples underscore the need for scientific accountability. Individuals who participate in studies, the scientific community, and broader society must have assurances that experiments are conducted in an ethical and responsible manner. Researchers must ensure that experiments (a) do not harm the individuals participating in them and (b) seek to maximize the possible benefits while simultaneously minimizing possible harms (The Belmont Report 1979; Gubler and Selway 2016).

Although political scientists in some subfields have long conducted public opinion surveys – which involve human respondents – for other subfields, research with human subjects is relatively new. Desposato (2016a) shows that there has been a dramatic increase in the use of experimental methods in political science over the past 20 years. In addition to experiments conducted in a university setting, political scientists increasingly incorporate experimental work in their field research, including research conducted abroad (Fujii 2012; Bhattacharya 2014; Desposato 2016; Cronin-Furman and Lake 2018; Knott 2019).

Note also that ethical and responsible practices regarding human subjects research is not only a matter for researchers using experimental methods. Schwartz-Shea and Yanow (2016) point out that US regulations indicate that any research that involves human subjects, defined as living human beings with whom the researcher communicates to obtain information for a study, must demonstrate that their work conforms to the relevant guidelines. They note that the regulations focus primarily on interpersonal contact, but that "identifiable private information" obtained from existing records or through internet searches may also be subject to IRB review (Schwartz-Shea and Yanow 2016: 279).

The purpose of such review is to ensure that research involving human subjects, irrespective of the specific research methodology, is conducted in a responsible manner. The Belmont Report enumerates three ethical principles that should guide research: (1) respect for persons, which requires that "subjects enter into the research voluntarily and with adequate information" (The Belmont Report 1979: 4); (2) beneficence, which entails an obligation to protect human subjects from harm and to secure their well-being. As mentioned above, this means adhering to two general rules: (a) do not harm and (b) maximize benefits while minimizing possible harm (The Belmont Report 1979; Gubler and Selway 2016); (3) justice, which requires that the researcher is mindful of "just ways to distribute burdens and benefits" of the study and the knowledge it produces (The Belmont Report 1979: 5). This last issue is quite difficult to adequately assess and is generally beyond the scope of IRB approval in US institutions. We address this category of ethical considerations in the next section of this chapter.

The institutionalized review of human subjects research by IRBs in the USA focuses on compliance with federal government policy – consent and the avoidance of harm to the participant. The latter is usually defined strictly in terms of the risks and benefits posed by the study itself. The former is judged on the basis of the explanation the researcher provides to the participant about the nature of the study. The explanation should provide sufficient information for participants to determine whether or not they wish to volunteer for the study – and avoid misleading them.

The IRB approval process is often risk-averse in an effort to avoid violating the relevant laws and regulations (Levine and Skedsvold 2008; Schwartz-Shea and Yanow 2016). However, there is also substantial variation in the interpretation of those laws and regulations, leading to variability in IRB review processes across institutions in the USA (Levine and Skedsvold 2008; Schwartz-Shea and Yanow 2016).

Internationally there is variability as well. The existence of institutionalized research oversight is by no means universal, but there is a growing list of countries with standards for human subjects research – as evidenced by a listing of standards for social and behavioral research provided by the Office for Human Research Protections (OHRP 2018). Researchers in countries that do not require IRB approval or a comparable process face greater difficulties in demonstrating that their work follows ethical standards and responsible research practices, because they cannot provide a journal with a letter or form that indicates their study has been vetted by such a board. Although the IRB process in the USA has been criticized for reducing research ethics to obtaining IRB approval (Fujii 2012), the absence of such an institution means that there is not a standard process by which scholars can demonstrate to journals that they have paid attention to these matters. And journals increasingly ask scholars to show that their research was approved by an IRB or an equivalent process for scholars based outside the USA.

Although journal editors are not "ethics sheriffs" (Wilson et al. 2016), they also have an incentive to ensure that the articles they publish report on research that has been conducted according to responsible research practices. Providing evidence of IRB approval – or an equivalent process – is helpful in this regard. However, as discussed in the next section, research ethics involves additional, thorny questions that are less easily resolved.

3.5 ETHICAL CONSIDERATIONS THAT IRB'S CANNOT ADDRESS

The process of obtaining IRB (or equivalent) approval customarily takes place before researchers embark on the quest to gather data from human subjects. Although this approval process is an important aspect of scientific accountability, it has a specific focus and does not cover all aspects of responsible research practices. The IRB approval process tends to focus on the design and administration of the study (Fujii 2012).

The process ascertains that researchers (1) have a clear plan for obtaining the voluntary consent of human subjects; (2) provide adequate information about the study so subjects can evaluate the risks and benefits of participating, and (3) have carefully designed the study to avoid harming human participants while maximizing the potential for gaining knowledge from the study (The Belmont Report 1979).

This last issue, the benefit versus harm consideration, is usually operationalized narrowly within the context of the experiment or interview protocol itself. This focus may be adequate for behavioral experiments conducted in laboratory settings in the USA and other global North contexts. However, political scientists increasingly conduct experiments and interviews during fieldwork abroad, often in conflict, post-conflict, and other fragile or dynamic settings (Fujii 2012; Bhattacharya 2014; Desposato 2016; Cronin-Furman and Lake 2018; Knott 2019).

These settings require additional considerations that are frequently ignored (Desposato 2016a; Cronin-Furman and Lake 2018). First, Desposato (2016b: 267) writes that IRBs in the USA have "generously approved" studies that researchers planned to administer outside the USA – and often in global South countries – that violated the laws of the locality where the experiments were conducted. Among the offenses committed as part of approved experimental designs, Desposato describes researchers and their confederates (i.e., persons helping the researchers implement the study) committing "traffic violations, soliciting and paying bribes, and violating electoral laws" (2016b: 267; Desposato 2016a provides further details). He compares these studies with the so-called Montana Study conducted in the USA. This study sought to identify "how providing information about candidates would affect participation" in a judicial election and was widely vilified (Desposato 2016b: 268). He notes that the Montana Study was less misleading than some of the studies that had been conducted outside the USA, including a study that distributed campaign flyers during an election in Brazil – a violation of local law (Desposato 2016a; 2016b).

This suggests that IRB approval does not guarantee that a study meets either ethical standards or remains within the legal parameters in the locality where it is administered. IRB approval provides only a partial check. Researchers still have a responsibility to carefully consider the tradeoffs between benefit and harm, as well as the social value the study may produce (Desposato 2016b). For research conducted internationally, an added question is whether the locale where the study is conducted will benefit from the knowledge gained through the study – a matter of the just distribution of burdens and benefits (The Belmont Report 1979).

Further, power differentials matter. Desposato (2016b: 267) concludes that researchers from the USA (or any other global North country) have a responsibility to consider how their perceived status might prevent local research assistants, confederates and participants "from speaking up about inappropriate interventions." One strategy is to check whether there are local protocols for research with human subjects and, if so, to ensure adherence to them (Desposato 2016b). In addition – and especially if there is no regulatory framework – researchers can learn about practices and laws by actively inviting the input from local collaborators to better understand how tradeoffs between benefit and harm might be understood by research participants (Fujii 2012).

Second, IRB approval processes are silent on the potential harms involved in publishing data gathered in conflict, post-conflict, and other fragile or dynamic settings. A manuscript may benefit from a few poignant quotes to highlight the key findings of the study, but even if subjects have given their consent, it may be wise to reflect carefully on the wisdom of revealing certain details. Fujii (2012) cautions researchers to think not only about the selection of pseudonyms for interview subjects, but also about the use of descriptive details about persons, the settings where interviews took place, and so on. An important consideration is whether such details are germane to the argument. Here, too, a thorough understanding of local conditions at the research site can facilitate making sound choices. Fujii (2012: 722) notes that responsible research practices include an effort to "anticipate how various audiences use [your] published work and take necessary precautions." While she acknowledges that it is not possible to control how others use your work, she argues that careful decisions about the use of data gathered through fieldwork can serve to minimize the potential harm to research participants and interview subjects (Fujii 2012).

Fieldwork based on interviews, while also subject to IRB approval, differs fundamentally from experimental work. The results of experiments are usually communicated in terms of aggregate statistics, whereas research based on interviews invites the use of descriptive information and evocative quotes. Hence, the latter may heighten the need to consider who might read the article and what consequences may result from the potential identification of subjects.

Third, researchers frequently work with local research assistants when conducting fieldwork. However, when publishing their work, such assistance is rarely acknowledged. This prompts Cronin-Furman and Lake (2018: 611) to argue that research partners and assistants in the global South "are rendered invisible at publication," a fact that "rarely catches the attention of editors or reviewers."

Ethical publication practices require that all who have contributed substantially to the paper should be acknowledged as authors, as discussed in the final section of Chapter 1. The failure to include persons who have made significant contributions was defined there as ghost authorship. It may be tempting to take full credit – especially when career advancement is on the line and research assistants reside in remote locales – but responsible publication practices demand that you acknowledge the roles of others in the production of each specific manuscript.

It is quite difficult for journal editors and reviewers to identify that co-authors have been ghosted and that research assistants remain unacknowledged. This makes it impossible for journal editors to effectively police this issue (Wilson et al. 2016). However, this does not give scholars license to exclude from co-authorship or other acknowledgment those who have made substantial contributions to their work. On the contrary, scholars do well to keep diligent records of the contributions made by research partners and assistants, whether at home or abroad. In doing so, scholars need to be mindful of power differentials that may make it difficult for such partners and assistants to broach the topic of co-authorship, and endeavor to be inclusive when considering who counts as a co-author or whose contributions need to be acknowledged.

Ethics and integrity in publishing is a complicated and multifaceted subject. Although academic journals increasingly establish policies to foster transparency (the subject of Chapter 4), responsible research practices still depend to a large degree on individual integrity. The pressure to publish may invite a temptation to take shortcuts, but the penalties for unethical conduct, when discovered, are substantial. Hence, responsible conduct in research and publication is the better long-term strategy for a sustained career as a scholar.

NOTES

1. This section relies substantially on Roig (2015), who provides a detailed account of the various forms of plagiarism and guidelines for avoiding it.
2. Nissani (1990) accepts the questionable ethics of the Milgram experiments, but offers an alternative explanation for the participants' behavior.

4. Research transparency across different types of scholarship

This chapter provides an overview of the principles of "research transparency," a principle to which major political science and international relations associations – such as the American Political Science Association (APSA) and the International Studies Association (ISA) have pledged support. This chapter explains how to meet the research transparency requirements, including replication standards for quantitative studies, of journals in both disciplines. We also illustrate strategies for making qualitative work conform to the emerging requirements of research transparency.

Both of this book's authors are deeply familiar with the issues related to transparency, since we instituted the current standard for research transparency for the APSR. The chapter examines the evolving debate over a "research transparency" or "reproducibility" standard and clarifies how this translates for quantitative and qualitative research.

We live in an era of research transparency. This is broadly defined as providing explicit and clear information about how your research was conducted so that another scholar could replicate your study. As a scholar preparing a manuscript for publication, you should anticipate this need for transparency and should also be prepared to share and make public some of your research materials and data. There has been much discussion on the importance of research transparency via replication studies in most of the social sciences in recent years, political science and international relations included. Indeed, the discussion on replication has become much more serious, as the entire landscape of publishing has changed in the past decade or so (Freese 2007; Gherghina and Katsanidou 2013). With the enormous expansion in data availability and the more prevalent requirement to share datasets, the opportunities to verify the findings of studies published in the discipline's major journals have also expanded.

The mantra has become "replication, replication" not only in political science and international relations, but also in other social sciences (such as economics, psychology and quantitative sociology). These developments have led to a debate about how to best "guard the high standards of research practice and allow for the maximum use of current knowledge for the further development of science" (Gherghina and Katsanidou 2013: 1; for similar sentiments, see King 1995).

Some advocates of greater research transparency via replication studies (e.g., King 2003) have even provided guidelines for what should be included in publicly available replication files. We address such requirements, as well as the reasons behind their emergence and the rationale for them, in this chapter.

4.1   WHAT IS REPLICATION AND TRANSPARENCY AND WHY DO IT?

Over the past 30 years there has been a push in political science and international relations to embrace efforts to reproduce empirical findings, which has often been equated with an emphasis on "replication." For instance, King (1995) has long championed the adoption of replication or reproducibility standards in the discipline. He argued that improving the possibilities for reproducibility will better enable scholars to "understand, evaluate, and build upon a prior work" (King 1995: 444). In 2014, the APSA drafted guidelines to encourage replication (or reproducibility of results) by emphasizing that researchers must provide (1) data access, (2) details of how they collected the data, and (3) details of the analysis that led to their conclusions (Lupia and Elman 2015).

However, there are different ways to think about "replication" (Janz 2016; Janz and Freese 2020). Replication can be thought of as the process by which a published article's findings are reanalyzed to confirm or disconfirm the results. How exactly such a replication study should be conducted, however, is still an open question (Carsey 2014: 73). As discussed in Chapter 2, some journals in the discipline now require that authors share their data and code, and confirm the accuracy of the analysis presented in a conditionally accepted manuscript. Although this can be considered replication, it is not the only way to define it.

Carsey (2014) and Janz (2016) identify three main questions with regard to replication: (1) Should the same, similar, or newly collected data be used? (2) How closely should one follow the original models? (3) How far should the new results deviate from the original work before claiming that the replication "failed"? Although all three approaches can be thought of as "replication" they are in fact quite different. The first approach – using the same data and models – is best defined as "reproducibility" or "duplication" studies. This is now a common standard for an increasing number of journals for quantitative analysis. These efforts involve using the same data and the original models to reproduce (or fail to reproduce) the empirical findings of the authors. This approach ensures that, using the same data and scripts that the author(s) used to produce the results reported in the manuscript, the same results are indeed produced. In other words, it allows journals to verify and check the results presented in the paper.

Janz (2016: 392) notes that reproducibility is "the gold standard for scientific research." The legitimacy of published work depends on whether we can replicate the analysis and reach the same results. Therefore, authors must provide information on how exactly they collected and analyzed their data. Without such transparency, scholars cannot fully understand the value of results and create new knowledge (King 1995). Reproducibility or duplication studies help to hold the original author "accountable" for their work, thereby acting as a "deterrent" for "irresponsible behavior" (Ishiyama 2014: 79).

More recently there has been a real push for research transparency that includes not only quantitative studies, but qualitative work as well. This effort to expand the concept of research transparency to include qualitative studies has had both advocates and opponents. Research transparency is defined as "making visible both the empirical foundation and the logic of inquiry of research" (Lupia and Elman 2015: 1). The idea of – and perceived need for – greater research transparency led to the development of a statement issued by a number of journal editors in 2015 that advocated for the advantages of greater data sharing and research transparency. This statement, signed by dozens of journal editors, declared a commitment to ensure that authors:

1. Make cited data available at the time of publication through a trusted digital repository.
2. Delineate clearly the analytic procedures upon which their published claims rely and, where possible, provide access to all relevant analytic materials.

Further, academic journals committed to establishing consistent data citation policies to ensure that data creators and suppliers receive appropriate credit for their work and that journal style guides, codes of ethics, publication manuals, and other forms of guidance are updated and expanded to include guidance regarding these improved data access and research transparency requirements.

In short, journals in political science and international relations have broadly adopted guidelines to promote research transparency. However, a question that has emerged in recent years is: who should be responsible for the enforcement of "transparency rules?" Although there has been a broad understanding in quantitative research in the discipline that provision of replication files is a positive development, there has been some debate over what is the best way to accomplish this, as well as what should be the role of journals in promoting this as a part of their editorial policies.

Although there have been advocates for the adoption of replication standards in political science and international relations since the 1990s (see King 1995; for a criticism of replication, see Gibson 1995), early efforts focused on only quantitative analysis and the provision of replication data. King (1995; 2003) proposed a "replication standard" for political scientists, which holds that sufficient information must exist with which to understand, evaluate and build upon a prior work so that a third party can replicate the results without any additional information from the author. Meeting the replication standard did not require any work to actually be replicated. It only required that sufficient information be provided so that the results could be replicated in principle. Indeed, journals like the *American Political Science Review* and the *Journal of Politics* adopted such replication policies in the earlier part of the twenty-first century and required that authors provide access to their data for replication purposes. However, the responsibility was entirely on the author to provide public access to data.

In recent years, the idea that there should be more of a "social" or "community" model of collective responsibility has been advocated by several scholars (King 2006; Freese 2007; Ishiyama 2014). Whereas the individualistic model holds that the primary responsibility for making available data for replication purposes lies with the individual author, the social or community model includes the provision that replication data be made available as a normal part of the publication process. This means that journals should require that the data be made available either as an online appendix provided by the journal or by a link, published by the journal, to a publicly accessible data repository. Thus, it is the responsibility of the journal as the representative of the scholarly community to ensure that data for replication purposes is provided to the broader scholarly community in an easily and broadly accessible manner.

Many argue that the community model does have some important advantages (e.g., Freese 2007). First, under a policy enforced by the journals, readers can expect that the author of an article has already provided data for replication purposes, whereas under the individualistic model the reader would have to trust that the author would provide the reader with data for replication upon request. Further, the social model of replication data provision also guarantees that data are provided in a fully reproducible manner and will be preserved over time. On the other hand, the individualistic model requires reliance on the ability and willingness of individual scholars to preserve replicable data. This may or may not happen, depending on the care a scholar takes to file data in an easily retrievable manner, as well as their responsiveness to requests. And, let's face it, scholars may lose files over the span of their careers. In other words, the "social policy seeks to decouple the content of articles from the contingencies of authors' futures" (Freese 2007: 156).

Finally, there is also something very practical regarding the promotion of the widespread proliferation of replication studies: the prospect that work will be replicated serves to promote greater scholarly honesty in terms of research. The pressure to produce "positive results" provides all sorts of incentives for "cooking" or "massaging" the data and results. In the worst-case scenario, this leads to falsification of data and/or findings, as illustrated in Chapter 3. Knowing that their work will be replicated and – perhaps even more importantly – that data and replication files will be made available for public scrutiny, encourages the original authors to be accountable for their work. In this way, the easy accessibility of replication files acts as a deterrent to unethical practices. We imagine that this will be true for qualitative work as well.

It should be noted, however, that the move towards the adoption of replication standards and data transparency has not been without its critics (e.g., Gherghina and Katsanidou 2013). For instance, Gibson (1995) has argued strongly against the introduction of journal enforced replication standards (the community model), suggesting that such a move would lead to a focus on minor methodological trivia and would minimize the value of the analysis of large secondary datasets in favor of small original ones. More importantly, there have been significant criticisms of the application of the "replication standard" to qualitative work.

Some have argued that the replication standard for quantitative work can be applied analogously to most qualitative research. For instance, King (1995) contends that a replication dataset for qualitative projects could include detailed descriptions of decision rules followed, interviews conducted, and information collected. Transcripts of interviews, photographs or audio tapes can readily be digitized and included in a replication dataset. Although he acknowledges that adhering to the replication standard is more difficult in qualitative research and sometimes cannot be completely followed, he considers it worthwhile for qualitative researchers to discuss collectively the appropriate applications or modifications of the replication standard (see Griffin and Ragin 1994; King 1995: 444).

After many years of discussion, some professional associations in political science and international relations have implemented requirements for the provision of replication materials to journals. In 2003, several major international relations journals introduced requirements for the provision of replication files as a condition for publication. These replication files are posted publicly. This was a direct result of a symposium on "Replication in International Studies Research" organized by one of the association's journals, *International Studies Perspectives* (Boyer 2003). As a result of these efforts, four leading international relation journals adopted a single common replication policy that applied to articles accepted by – and published in – *International Studies Quarterly*, the *Journal of Peace Research*, the *Journal of Conflict Resolution* and *International Interactions* (James 2003; Gleditsch et al. 2003a; Gleditsch et al. 2003b).

One of these journals was the flagship journal of the ISA, *International Studies Quarterly*. Its submission guidelines clearly state the requirement that authors make "their data ... fully accessible. If the data in question are not already publicly archived, authors will be required to certify that the data are readily available to others. Requests for copies of the data must be addressed to the author or authors, and not the offices of ISQ." Thus, there is no requirement that data be deposited with ISQ, as is the case with the *American Journal of Political Science* (AJPS), as long as the author can document that it is publicly archived elsewhere. If not, data are archived with the journal and made available on the ISA's website. These journals, however, have no specific guidelines regarding the provision of transparency materials for qualitative research.

On the other hand, the APSA moved in the direction of establishing guidelines for promoting research transparency for both quantitative and qualitative research. In 2012, the APSA Executive Council approved new language on transparency and replicability in the *APSA Guide to Professional Ethics in Political Science*. Subsequently, a "Data Access and Research Transparency" (DA-RT) committee, working on its own, held meetings and sessions at annual conventions and hosted a special conference on DA-RT. In 2014, editors from some APSA section journals and the APSR made a commitment to implement strategies for research transparency, in principle for both quantitative and qualitative work. Since then, editors of some non-APSA political science journals have implemented guidelines and, after convening working groups and consulting with its Editorial Board to help refine their own version, the APSR editors promulgated draft guidelines to govern both quantitative and qualitative research. These went into effect in January 2016.

There have been many skeptics regarding DA-RT, particularly with reference to how the "replication standard" could or should be applied to qualitative research (see Schwartz-Shea and Yanow 2016). Given the variety of different kinds of work that together fit under the umbrella of qualitative work, many point out that the development of a single standard for such scholarship is not realistic. Others raise questions about ethical concerns, such as making interview transcripts, photographs or audio tapes public, which runs the risk of compromising the identities of interviewees. This, in turn, may jeopardize the safety and security of the individuals involved, leading to ethical questions as discussed in the final section of Chapter 3. These issues have weighed heavily on discussions regarding the application of DA-RT principles relating to the publication of qualitative work in political science and international relations journals.

4.2 WHAT DO JOURNALS REQUIRE FOR REPRODUCIBILITY?

Although many journals have adopted guidelines to promote research transparency, there is a good deal of variation in terms of what is required for submission, particularly with regard to quantitative and qualitative research. In this section, we will first focus on quantitative research, discussing two issues: what should the author be generally prepared to provide to meet the replication and transparency requirements for journals, and when should authors be expected to provide such materials?

4.2.1   Quantitative Research

Before discussing what is to be provided to the journal for quantitative research, it is important to note that not all journals have adopted the "community" model for replication of quantitative studies. Indeed, many – if not most – journals, particularly specialized or "niche" journals that have smaller editorial staffs, tend to emphasize individual responsibility for the provision of data and code for replication and they do not enforce their replication policies. Many journals officially commit to the principles of DA-RT, but in practice have continued to simply require that the author commit to making data and code available. It is, however, a good idea for authors to check with the editorial instructions for journals to confirm the current policies of each journal regarding replication requirements.

Several top-ranked journals do require that data and code for the purposes of replication be provided by authors. Authors are generally expected to provide these materials *prior* to publication. Generally, this means that authors are expected to provide supplemental documents such as the data files used in the analysis and the program codes employed (e.g., STATA do-files, R-scripts, or an SPSS command file) after acceptance of the piece, but before publication (i.e., while the manuscript is *conditionally accepted*). Authors may also be asked to describe clearly where the original sources of data can be found and how variables were transformed, although for most journals it is acceptable to include such descriptions in the text of the article (Dafoe 2014). Further, these data are generally either deposited directly with the journal and made available as supplemental files on the journal's website (this is the case with journals associated with the International Studies Association) or made available in repositories such as the Dataverse Network at Harvard University, the Inter-university Consortium for Political and Social Research (ICPSR), or other persistent archives. Some journals allow the author to provide replication materials on their own website (Dafoe 2014). If data is proprietary or other nondisclosure agreements prohibit open access to the data that was used, this should be noted by the author(s) and they should provide a description of the procedures used to obtain access to the data (Carsey 2014; Lupia and Alter 2014; Lupia and Elman 2014).

A typical set of requirements of journals in the field is illustrated by the list of materials authors should submit prior to publication at the *American Political Science Review*. For quantitative research, the journal requires that data and relevant commands are deposited to the APSR dataverse. The materials deposited should allow for the reproduction of the results described in the text, as well as any appendix, unless legal, ethical or methodological constraints prevent such data sharing. There is no apparent requirement for the provision of command files that led to the production of the final dataset, such as merge files and recode commands, but that is implied.

Finally, authors should carefully and completely cite all data that were used either in the analysis itself or that led to the construction of the measurements of the variables. Such a citation should be provided at an appropriate point in the text of the article, and the citation should be listed in the reference section of their article, preferably using a persistent identifier such as a Digital Object Identifier (DOI).

Perhaps some of the most explicit and detailed guidelines are provided by the *American Journal of Political Science* (AJPS), one of the top-ranked political science journals in the world. The AJPS lists specific procedures for the preparation of replication files, which are consistent with the expectations that are laid out in the APSA's *A Guide to Professional Ethics in Political Science* (revised, 2012). This policy is "strict," which requires that authors of accepted articles provide the data and code necessary to reproduce the results. The journal itself ensures that the results are reproducible before the piece is published. The required files not only include the software command files to reproduce the results, but also the commands used to merge files, recode data, and produce the values that appear in the dataset used by the authors. Importantly, the replication materials are not provided for the review process but only for the purposes of verification once the author(s) has received a conditional accept decision. The AJPS houses all data at a dedicated dataverse site and there are detailed instructions provided to authors as to how to upload such data (see https://ajps.org/wp-content/uploads/2018/05/ajps_replication-guidelines-2-1.pdf).

The AJPS generally is an extreme example of very explicit guidelines for the provision of both quantitative and (qualitative) data for the purposes of reproducibility. More commonly, the requirements are less extensive. Box 4.1 provides a list of the supplementary files authors are typically expected to supply.

BOX 4.1   LIST OF SUPPLEMENTARY FILES TO BE SUBMITTED FOR REPLICATION PURPOSES: QUANTITATIVE RESEARCH

1. Dataset that is used for the study (authors are generally not required to submit all data, only the data used for the analysis – unless specified otherwise by the journal).
2. Relevant comments used to conduct the analysis (STATA do-files or R-scripts or an SPSS command file).
3. Rule of thumb: submit materials that allow other researchers to duplicate your findings.
4. Some journals (not all) require all commands used in variable transformation, recodes and computations. Authors should check with journal submission guidelines.

4.2.2   Qualitative Research

There is far less consensus on guidance regarding the reproducibility of qualitative work as compared to the requirements for quantitative scholarship. That said, some journals – most notably AJPS – have provided very explicit guidelines regarding the materials that should be provided prior to the publication of a qualitative piece. Most journals do not have such highly developed guidelines, but it is worth noting what might be required, because it gives some insight into what may be required of qualitative researchers in the future.

One of the great challenges in applying replication standards to qualitative analysis is that there is a great variety of research traditions that exist under the broad umbrella of qualitative work. Some approaches are more conducive to the replication guidelines that are comparable to those used for quantitative research. Although there remains considerable debate over whether a replication standard can (or should) be developed for qualitative analysis, some journals have developed guidelines that represent a potential glimpse as to what may emerge in the future. It is important for authors to be aware of the debates and possible future requirements. However, to meet current guidelines, authors should consult the specific guidelines regarding transparency for qualitative research provided by the journals to which they plan to submit their work.

Some journals, such as the AJPS, have provided detailed guidelines for submissions that use qualitative research techniques (see https://ajps .org/wp-content/uploads/2018/05/ajps_replication-guidelines-2-1.pdf). Although these guidelines do not mandate a strict replication standard for manuscripts using qualitative research techniques, in principle, authors are required to make their scholarship transparent and able to be evaluated. This involves a description of the research processes used and, where possible, the provision of the materials that were necessary to arrive at the findings and conclusions presented.

Two general categories of "qualitative forms" are discussed in these guidelines. First, there are manuscripts that use data organized in "matrix form," which is common for approaches such as Qualitative Comparative Analysis (QCA) or automated content analysis. The second are manuscripts that use the "granular form" of qualitative research, where information is drawn from the content of cited sources (e.g., book, interview, newspaper article, video clips), interviews with individual subjects or conversations with participants in focus groups as distinct inputs into the analysis.

As for the "matrix forms," such as automated content analysis, the guidelines suggest that author(s) describe in either the text or in an appendix the text collection procedure and (where possible) provide digital copies of the original full texts that were analyzed. If these texts are proprietary and/or if there are other ethical or legal restrictions on the sharing of such files, then the authors should explain what these restrictions are and how the texts could be accessed by other researchers. For QCA, authors should include a discussion of the code for the calibration of sets, the construction of truth tables, the minimization of truth tables, and the representation of the results. Further, authors should include information regarding the calibration function; a description of the consistency and frequency threshold, how logical remainders are treated and any other consideration (such as references to specific case knowledge) when truth tables are constructed. Box 4.2 provides a list of files journals may wish to see for "matrix forms" of qualitative research.

BOX 4.2 LIST OF SUPPLEMENTARY FILES FOR "MATRIX" FORMS OF QUALITATIVE RESEARCH (E.G., AUTOMATED CONTENT ANALYSIS AND QCA)

Authors should include in either the appendix or text:

1. For content analysis, a description of the text collection procedure and (where possible) provide digital copies of the original full texts that were analyzed.
2. For QCA, a discussion of the code for the calibration of sets, construction of truth tables, the minimization of truth tables, and the representation of the results.
3. For QCA, authors should include information regarding the calibration function; a description of the consistency and frequency threshold, how logical remainders are treated and any other consideration (such as reference to specific case knowledge) when truth tables are constructed.

For "granular forms" of qualitative research, which include archival work, detailed case studies using secondary materials, and field interviews, the guidelines suggest the creation of a "Transparency Appendix" or TRAX. According to Moravcsik, Elman and Kapiszewski (2013), a TRAX comprises two sections, an overview section and a set of annotations called active citation (see https://qdr.syr.edu/ati/guide-ati). The first section should provide a brief summary of the author's research trajectory, describing the context, design, and conduct of research. This part should also outline the source collection and data generation processes employed in the article, including a statement regarding the sources that were used.

The second section of the TRAX consists of annotations that enhance, as necessary, the discussion of the connections between data, analysis and empirical claims that are offered in the text. This involves:

a. A precise and complete reference, with all information that scholars would need to locate the cited source.
b. Excerpts from cited sources, typically 100 to 150 words from a textual source. For handwritten material, audiovisual material, or material generated through interviews or focus groups, include an excerpt

from the transcription. If there are restrictions on the use of excerpts from source subjects (such as ethical concerns about revealing identities of those interviewed), copyright or logistical constraints, then authors should provide an explanation of those restrictions and (if necessary) a redaction of the relevant text.

c. Analytic notes that illustrate how the data were generated from the sources to support empirical claims should be accessible in some way – either described in the text or provided in the appendix.

For further guidance on producing a TRAX, a very useful source is provided by the Qualitative Data Repository website (see https://qdr.syr.edu/content/trax-conversion-instructions).

A somewhat different approach is offered by the APSR. Rather than lay out specific detailed guidelines on what to submit for qualitative work, the APSR offers more flexibility in submissions, emphasizing that the author comply with the ethics and transparency guidelines provided in two documents: the APSA's *A Guide to Professional Ethics in Political Science* (2012) and the *Principles and Guidance for Human Subjects Research* (approved by the APSA Council, April 4, 2020). The latter was adopted in reaction to concerns that the DA-RT guidelines adopted by many journals did not include adequate provisions to protect the identities of human subjects included in qualitative studies. A concern was that journals would require scholars to make confidential information available for public scrutiny, forcing scholars to violate professional ethics. Hence, for the APSR, what is required for qualitative work is that upon conditional acceptance for publication, authors (especially those whose work directly engages human participants in the research process) are required to:

• Affirm a set of ethical and/or transparency declarations related to these principles.
• Submit an appendix that explains any exceptions or issues related to the above principles, revised (if relevant) in light of comments from reviewers and editors.
• Further, additional relevant additional documents should be included, such as (but not limited to):
    1. Ethics certificates or approvals from all organizations that approved the research.
    2. Other research documentation, such as interview guides.

In sum, there are a variety of guidelines for journal articles using qualitative research, ranging from offering very little or no guidance on transparency for qualitative work (which is the majority of current journals in political science and international relations) to very specific guidelines (as illustrated by those provided by the AJPS) and everywhere in between. The best advice to authors is to be prepared to demonstrate transparency by documenting everything you can document about your research process and to consult the author guidelines of the journal to which you plan to submit your work. If the guidelines are not clear, it may be worthwhile to communicate directly with the editors in an effort to understand what, specifically, their transparency guidelines are for qualitative work. Box 4.3 provides useful links for learning more about developments in transparency requirements for granular forms of qualitative research.

BOX 4.3 USEFUL LINKS FOR TRANSPARENCY MATERIALS FOR "GRANULAR" FORMS OF QUALITATIVE RESEARCH

For general guidance on qualitative research transparency, see:

1. Qualitative Data Repository website: https://qdr.syr.edu.
2. Moravcsik's (2019) book: https://www.princeton.edu/~amoravcs/ library/TransparencyinQualitativeResearch.pdf.
3. Kapiszewski and Karcher's (2019) article: https://preprints .apsanet.org/engage/api-gateway/apsa/assets/orp/resource/item/ 5d94c7762f41c7001256af6d/original/transparency-in-practice-in -qualitative-research.pdf.
4. For "active citation" annotations, see Elman et al. (2017): https:// qdr.syr.edu/ati/guide-ati.
5. For development of TRAX files, see https://qdr.syr.edu/content/ trax-conversion-instructions.

4.2.3   Preregistration

In recent years, as part of the move towards greater research transparency, there has also been a growing amount of attention paid to "pre-registration" or "registration" of research studies prior to publication. Registration of research studies essentially means that even before engaging in the analysis of the data, researchers publicly release their hypotheses and plan for data analysis. Several scholars have argued in favor of registration in the social sciences in general and political science in particular (King et al. 2007; 2009; Humphreys et al. 2013; Monogan 2013; 2015).

Proponents of preregistering a project argue that this will reduce the likelihood of *publication bias*, which is the tendency for positive results to be favored in publication over studies that produce null or negative findings. There is some evidence of such biases in political science articles and it presumably exists among international relations scholarship as well (Gerber and Malhotra 2008; Gerber et al. 2010).

Monogan (2015) and Gerber and Malhotra (2008) identify four potential causes for publication bias: (1) Attempts to publish null findings often lead to rejection of the relevant manuscript; (2) Authors may self-select to submit only studies with significant and positive results; (3) "Fishing," which includes both an author's expansion of samples after failing significance tests, and (4) Authors searching for different analytical techniques to generate significant results (Gerber and Malhotra 2008: 314). By preregistering studies, advocates argue, these biases can be eliminated.

However, there have also been detractors of the push for preregistration, which was envisioned by its advocates as an approach that could be used across political science and international relations. Most notably, Laitin (2013) argued that although registration may work well for clinical research where the incentives are strong for "positive results," this does not apply to fields that are based on observational data. Indeed, Laitin raises the issue that some of the most important developments in political science and international relations have come from inductive studies. He notes that studies often evolve and change over time, with a cycle between theory and learning from the data. Thus, in his view, preregistration is ill-suited for the research strategies that are most common in our discipline. Anderson (2013) echoes some of these concerns when he notes that, although registration might be useful for some experimental studies (which are gaining currency in the social sciences), they are ill-suited for the analysis of historical or secondary data. Like Laitin, he also contends that discouraging the evolution of one's thinking about observed empirical relationships can be detrimental to scientific development in the field.

As a result of these concerns, most journals do not require preregistration in general. However, some, such as the *Journal of Politics* (JOP), do explicitly require preregistration for certain kinds of studies. In particular, JOP requires preregistration of submitted manuscripts that contain original experimental work. This requirement applies not only to laboratory experiments, but also to field and survey experiments. These studies are required to submit proof of preregistration with one of the existing research registries (e.g., EGAP, RCT, Open Science). JOP does encourage, but does not require, the preregistration of other types of research designs. Submission of unregistered laboratory, field and survey experiments are not accepted – and will lead to desk rejection. This policy was introduced only recently and 2021 is considered a transition year during which authors seeking to be grandfathered into the old requirements (i.e., no preregistration) must write to the editors for permission to do so.

Many other journals either do not require preregistration or merely encourage it. For instance, *Comparative Political Studies* (CPS) indicates that authors may provide an anonymized version of a preregistration plan, but they are not required to do so and are not required to register the plan with one of the existing research registries.

Although preregistration is considered part of the effort to encourage research transparency in journal article publication, it remains largely limited to studies that employ clinical or field experiments, and is generally not required for most other types of research in political science and international relations. That said, as with much of what we discuss in this book, authors should be aware of the debates and the possible future directions of publication requirements in the discipline's journals.

4.3   REPLICATION STUDIES

Another possible outlet for publication that has arisen as the result of a greater emphasis on replication and reproducibility is the publication of *replication studies*. Indeed, Ishiyama (2014) and Janz and Freese (2020) argue that if political science and international relations aspire to raise the degree of scientific rigor in their respective fields some venue should exist to publish replication studies. This would incentivize the development of what Robert Merton (1973 [1942]) called "organized skepticism" as a necessary condition for the development of an effective science.

Replication studies go beyond simple verification of the results, based upon the data and code provided by the authors. Replication projects, according to Janz and Freese (2020) are really extensions of published work that interrogate the sturdiness of the work's findings. What is commonly thought of as replication is in fact verification, and was called duplication by King (1995: 451) and is currently often discussed as reproducibility. Verification seeks to confirm the results reported in a published work, whereas replication projects are efforts to elaborate findings or increase their scope beyond duplication.

Many published journal articles are replications in the sense that they are extensions and elaborations that examine the sturdiness of the reported results by reexamining the original data used and/or using different model specifications. In a recent article, Janz and Freese (2020: 2) offer a very useful set of guidelines to produce "constructive" replications studies. They point to two examples to illustrate these types of studies. Gerber and Green (2000) published an article in the *American Political Science Review* using a field experiment that demonstrated that voter turnout increased after personal canvassing but did not increase after voters received telephone calls. A later study replicated the original findings (also published in the APSR) and reported that the authors' negative finding was really "caused by inadvertent deviations from their stated experimental protocol," pointing to "systematic patterns of implementation errors" (Imai 2005: 283). The original authors then replied to Imai, stating that the replication contained "statistical, computational, and reporting errors that invalidate its conclusions"; that the original Gerber and Green study had made mistakes; and claiming that "none of the key substantive or methodological claims of Professor Imai's essay survives scrutiny" (Gerber and Green 2005: 301).

Another example is the replication of an article by Peffley et al. (2001a) on citizens' political tolerance. The study was replicated by Miller et al. (2001: 407), who found "significant differences when attempting to replicate" the original study. However, unlike Imai's critique of the Gerber and Green study, in this case the replicators showed how they double-checked their own procedures, saying they wanted to give the "original analyses the benefit of the doubt" (Miller et al. 2001: 408). After some scrutiny, they concluded that the authors of the original piece had made a simple coding error and that "these analysis errors are not significant enough to dismiss this article totally" (Miller et al. 2001: 409). In response, the original authors replied that the replication was itself flawed and that the replicators' criticisms were "seriously exaggerated" (Peffley et al. 2001b: 422).

As Janz and Freese (2020: 3) point out, in the second example, the authors of the replication study used slightly more positive language (although the response was rather sharp). This is in contrast to the first example, where the replicator adopted what could be perceived as an "accusatory" tone. Janz and Freese caution authors to be careful about the language they use. Although both examples illustrate good practices, such as using a detailed comparison of results, and investigating beyond the data and code provided (as is required for simple verification studies), they differed in terms of the interpretation of the importance of the differences in findings – and in the former case, this interpretation took a "personal and accusatory tone" (Janz and Freese 2020: 3).

Janz and Freese (2020: 1) argue – and we believe this to be sound advice – that authors who seek to conduct replication studies should view these as "intrinsically delicate endeavors." However, they are necessary to address a "crisis of credibility" that has provoked other developments in the natural and social sciences to promote "open science." As they point out:

> Achieving a research culture in which replications become more accepted and human errors are normalized involves cultivating principles by which replications can be undertaken in a maximally constructive way. This way, they become publishable (for the replicators) and there is nothing to fear (for the original authors). (Janz and Freese 2020: 3)

The publication of replication studies is also therefore an alternative for scholars to publish in the best journals in political science and international relations.

4.4   MOVING TOWARDS GREATER RESEARCH TRANSPARENCY IN PUBLISHED JOURNAL ARTICLES

In sum, in recent years there has been a greater push towards the promotion of research transparency by requiring authors to furnish materials to journals that help ensure the replicability of quantitative work and provide greater scrutiny of qualitative work. Despite some variation in terms of the code to be provided (whether the journal itself will seek to replicate the findings, or whether the journal requires deposit of data at their website or trusts the author to make the data publicly available), there is a growing consensus as to what materials are to be submitted to journals prior to the final acceptance of quantitative articles. There is considerably less consensus regarding the materials required for qualitative work. Although readers can expect the further evolution of replication standards over the coming years, at this point readers are strongly encouraged to investigate the transparency requirements of individual journals prior to submission of a manuscript. Given the variation that currently exists, it is wise to consult the author guidelines of specific journals before submitting a manuscript.

5. New frontiers in publishing: understanding open access journals

Publishing in the best academic journals has always been challenging. It has become even more difficult to navigate with the addition of open access and predatory publishing. These two newer phenomena in the world of academic publishing are not the same, but it can be difficult to discern the difference between them.

This chapter contrasts open access (OA) journal publishing with the more conventional subscription-based model to achieve a better understanding of the ways in which the two models work. Next, the chapter turns to an explanation of the different types of OA publishing – such as Gold OA and Green OA – before focusing its attention on predatory journals. The latter sometimes masquerade as OA journals and it is important to understand – and be able to spot – the difference. We close the chapter with a discussion of the costs and benefits of OA publishing for authors.

5.1 WHAT IS OPEN ACCESS?

Open access (OA) publishing differs from traditional journal publishing. Articles published in this way are freely available to anyone who wishes to read and/or download them. This is not the case for articles published in traditional academic journals, which can be accessed only by subscription. To understand OA, it is important to appreciate how traditional journal publishing works. Therefore, we first explain how scholars (and other readers) access articles published in traditional and OA journals, and then discuss differences in getting published in the two formats.

Most scholars (and students) access academic journals primarily through the library of their university or research institute. Many scholars also have access to some journals via membership in one or more professional societies – access to the association-sponsored journals is usually a benefit of membership. Further, it is possible to take out individual subscriptions, but this is not common, mostly because this tends to be quite expensive. Whether the subscription is institutional, a benefit of membership, or individual, in all these situations the content of these traditional journals is behind a "paywall." This means that anyone who does not have a subscription cannot access the journal's content – or must pay a fee for access to a specific article. By placing articles behind a paywall, this publication model places limits on the scope of individuals who can access the results of academic research.

Over the past several decades, university libraries in the USA and elsewhere have contended with both the rising cost and the proliferation of academic publications, both of which have placed a strain on their budgets (Atchison and Bull 2015). Libraries have been forced to make some difficult choices about which subscriptions to continue and which to cancel. To do this, librarians track the usage of different journals to help them evaluate which subscriptions are most important to keep. As a result, highly specialized publications that are of interest to very few scholars risk becoming less accessible – unless they are part of a "bundle" or a group of journals sold by a larger publisher as a package. Some of the larger publishing companies, which offer a broad range of journals, now require libraries to purchases bundles of journal subscriptions for a flat fee. Such bundles invariably include both widely read and very specialized publications. The side-effect of this bundling is that libraries are forced to maintain subscriptions to some highly specialized journals with very small readerships which are part of the bundle, while simultaneously creating gaps in their holdings of more widely read journals that are not part of such bundles. A related side-effect of bundling is also that librarians end up with less control over the decision regarding which subscriptions to continue. In other words, bundling reduces the ability of librarians to maintain collections that best serve the needs of the scholars at their institutions.

During this period of rising journal subscription costs and bundling, we also observe the emergence of a number of new academic journals in political science and international relations – both independent and sponsored by professional societies. For instance, the American Political Science Association (APSA) started *Perspectives on Politics* in 2003. Sections of the APSA started the *Journal of Political Science Education* and *Politics & Gender*, both in 2005. The International Studies Association also saw an expansion of its journal offerings. It launched five new journals between 1994 and 2016: *International Studies Review*, *International Studies Perspectives*, *Foreign Policy Analysis*, *International Political Sociology* and the *Journal of Global Security Studies*. This confluence of an increase in the number of journals and rising subscription costs combined with the distortions created by the bundling of subscriptions to create an opening for new publication models, such as OA (Atchison and Bull 2015).

The key argument in favor of OA publishing is that it makes academic research much more widely accessible, because journal content is no longer hidden behind a paywall. This access benefits scholars and students, as well as the general public. This argument is deemed especially important by government organizations that provide funding for research: if the research is paid for with public funds, then everyone – including the public – should be able to access the articles based on the work that was done with their money (Gleditsch 2012; Jisc 2019).

The impetus for open access is the principle that both scholars and society as a whole benefit from making the results of scientific studies openly accessible (see https://www.coalition-s.org/why-plan-s/). The idea was underwritten by a number of universities and funders in Europe, as is evident in the list of signatories of the Berlin Declaration of 2003 (see https://openaccess.mpg.de/Berlin-Declaration) and has coalesced in "Plan S" (https://www.coalition-s.org/). Plan S includes not only universities and funders; it has also received backing from governments in the European Union, ensuring that the landscape for scholarly publishing will indeed change, albeit slower than the 2020 target date and possibly with some modifications from the original plan. Although Plan S originates in Europe and affects European scholars in the first instance, political science and international relations are sufficiently international that these changes will affect scholars in many other locations as well.

Scholars benefit from OA publishing as consumers of research articles. Traditionally, the broadest range of journals was available at well-endowed research universities, where scholars benefitted from well-stocked libraries. Outside of those elite universities, access to journals has always been less comprehensive, because the libraries at other types of institutions always contended with smaller budgets. Arguments in favor of OA publishing often focus the debate on improving access for scholars in the global South (Gleditsch 2012; Mehlum 2012; Thompson 2012; Jisc 2019). Indeed, universities in the global South face even more acute budget constraints than smaller universities in the global North. In addition, exchange rates often make academic journals published in the USA or other global North countries prohibitively expensive. To mediate this problem, some of the larger journal publishing companies have developed programs to offer free access to scholars in the global South (Gleditsch 2012; Mehlum 2012; Morgan et al. 2012). That sounds promising, but such free access tends to be limited to scholars residing in countries that publishers perceive to hold no commercial potential (Mehlum 2012). The result is odd: scholars with access to well-endowed research libraries in the global North and those residing in the least-resourced parts of the global South have access, whereas those residing in middle-income countries have more limited – or no – access (Mehlum 2012). Scholars at smaller and/or teaching-focused universities in the USA and elsewhere face limits on access as well – although some of this problem is mediated through interlibrary loan schemes. Both the pressures on university library budgets in the global North and the problem of uneven access globally contribute to the attraction of OA publication models, because they make it possible for everyone with a computer and an internet connection to gain access to journal content (Atchison and Bull 2015).

OA publishing differs from traditional journal publishing with respect to how the costs associated with publishing are paid. Whereas traditional journals charge a subscription fee, OA journals do not. A common strategy to fund journal operations is through Article Processing Charges (APCs), which may be paid by the author, the funder of the research, or some other party (Jisc 2019). This other party could be a professional society that (partially) subsidizes APCs for its members or a foundation that funds the journal's operations (Morgan et al. 2012). For example, when *Research & Politics* was launched as a peer-reviewed OA journal in 2014, the publisher covered the APCs for the first two years and a grant from the Carnegie Corporation covered the APCs for the next two years. At this time, *Research & Politics* is maintaining its no-APCs policy. This will not be the case for all OA journals. For instance, when the ISA launched *Global Studies Quarterly* (GSQ) as an OA journal in 2021, it promised only that the APCs may be waived for scholars from the global South – suggesting that others will be asked to pay these charges.

The OA publishing model is still relatively new. Although there is a growing number of OA journals, many aspects of this publishing model remain unclear. The strategy followed by *Research & Politics* acknowledges the widespread aversion to "pay to publish," whereas GSQ's strategy may make it more difficult to develop the publication into a respected venue for quality scholarship.

In addition to fully OA journals, traditional journals increasingly offer scholars the option to publish their article OA as well (Calise et al. 2010; Atchison and Bull 2015). In the latter case, most of the journal's content will be behind the subscription paywall, but some articles are published OA if the author(s) choose to pay the associated APCs. Authors may choose to do this if the research was funded by an organization that requires the products of that research to be broadly accessible. Alternatively, authors may perceive an incentive to publish OA if they believe that publishing OA may result in a broader readership and additional citations of their work, *and* they have access to the necessary funds. This type of OA publishing is generally referred to as a "hybrid" model, because the journal remains a traditional subscription-based one but adds an option to make the article openly accessible for a fee. We discuss this further in the next section on different forms of OA.

As an author, your experience of submitting an article to a reputable OA journal should not differ substantially from the process at a traditional subscription-based journal. We emphasize "reputable," because the world of OA includes not only professional, peer-reviewed journals, but also predatory ones. We discuss this in a later section of this chapter.

Reputable OA journals follow the same conventions of double-blind peer review that are common to traditional subscription-based ones, as described in Chapter 2. The main difference is that the instructions for authors will include information on the APCs. Reputable OA journals will be transparent about APCs, as well as any available discounts or waivers. In addition, authors can check whether the journal is listed in the Directory of Open Access Journals (DOAJ), which offers a searchable database of OA journals that meet certain standards. For example, the instructions for authors on the publisher's webpage announce that the APCs for *Political Research Exchange* (PRX), launched in 2019 as a fully open access journal, are supported by a subsidy from the European Consortium for Political Research (ECPR), its sponsoring professional society. The DOAJ provides the same information.

OA publishing has gained in popularity, but it is not yet clear to what extent it will replace the traditional subscription model (Nentwich 2008; Calise et al. 2010; Mehlum 2012). However, the OA model's presence in the world of academic journal publishing makes it important to understand. Next, we explain in more detail the different forms of OA.

5.2   WHAT ARE THE DIFFERENT FORMS OF OPEN ACCESS?

OA publishing takes several different forms. Each comes with different rights for the author and the publisher, as well as different ways to defray the costs of publishing. The discussion in the previous section has focused primarily on so-called Gold OA. However, this is not the only form OA can take. Here, we describe the different types of OA and introduce some of the Creative Commons licenses associated with OA publishing. The latter specify the terms of use of the material published under each particular type of license.

First, articles published as Gold OA will be freely available to anyone who wishes to read them as soon as they are published. Gold OA articles can be published in either OA journals or traditional subscription-based ones. As discussed in the previous section, the main difference between these two types of journals is how the costs associated with publishing are covered. Traditional journals derive their income from subscriptions, whereas OA journals depend on income from Article Processing Charges (APCs). These APCs are charged to the author(s), who can sometimes build them into a grant or find another party – such as their university – to pay these costs (Jisc 2019). A professional society may (partially) subsidize APCs for its members or a foundation may provide a grant to fund an OA journal's operations (Morgan et al. 2012). Such grants or subsidies may result in reduced or no APC costs for authors. Whichever is the case, the article is freely available to any and all readers. Hence, anyone with an internet connection and an interest in the subject matter can go to the OA journal's webpage, and read or download the articles available there. There is no paywall, as is the case with subscription-based journals.

Subscription-based journals increasingly offer scholars the option to publish their article OA as well (Calise et al. 2010; Atchison and Bull 2015). This is often referred to as a "hybrid" model. The subscription-based journal continues to rely primarily on income from subscriptions. Authors are not required to pay, but if they do so, their article is made available to anyone who wishes to access it, rather than to only the subscribers of the journal. The fee paid to a hybrid journal is technically not an APC, because the article will be published irrespective of payment. Instead, the payment reflects a "rights transaction" that makes the specific article more widely available than the content for which the additional fee has not been paid (Morgan et al. 2012: 230).

Subscription-based journals may indicate OA content with a logo that resembles an open padlock, as illustrated in Box 5.1, although the same logo is often also used to indicate to subscribers that they have access to this content. The logo was originally introduced as a symbol of open access by the Public Library of Science (PLOS), a non-profit that advocates for this type of publishing and produces a series of OA journals.

BOX 5.1   OPEN ACCESS LOGO

Second, Green OA is sometimes also referred to as "self-archiving" and pertains to articles that were published in subscription-based journals (Jisc 2019). Self-archiving means that scholars make their work accessible beyond the subscribers to the journal in which it is published. This can be done by placing a version of the article on their personal website or in some repository, such as one maintained by a scholar's university library (Calise et al. 2010; Morgan et al. 2012; Atchison and Bull 2015).

Subscription-based journals differ in the rights to self-archiving they grant their authors. Some are very permissive and others quite restrictive. The most permissive Green OA privileges allow scholars to self-archive any version of their article, although usually after an embargo period, whereas the most restrictive limit self-archiving to something they call the "pre-print" version (Atchison and Bull 2015; Jisc 2019). There is confusion over what "pre-print" means. In the context of Green OA, publishers usually define it as the version of the paper *before* peer review, i.e., the version that was initially submitted rather than the one that was revised on the basis of the reviews (Atchison and Bull 2015; Jisc 2019). Depending on the extent of the revisions made, the pre-print can differ substantially from the final, published version.

It is easy to be confused about your rights as an author under Green OA, because there is so much variation in the self-archiving policies of different journals and publishers. This may be a reason why relatively few authors take advantage of the self-archiving options that are legally available to them (Morgan et al. 2012; Atchison and Bull 2015). To better understand whether you may self-archive – and which version of your article to select – consult the Sherpa Romeo database (Jisc 2020). This database is freely accessible online at https://v2.sherpa.ac.uk/romeo/ and provides information on whether, and with what conditions, you may self-archive the submitted version, the accepted version, and the published version.

For instance, the Sherpa Romeo database entry for the *American Political Science Review* notes that scholars are free to self-archive their submitted version (but must note acceptance for publication), may post the accepted version as soon as it has been accepted for publication, and must pay an additional fee to self-archive the published version. In other words, in order to make the published version freely accessible, the author is required to pay the Gold OA fee. Another example is the Sherpa Romeo entry for *Acta Politica*, which allows authors to self-archive their submitted version, but places a twelve-month embargo on the accepted version and an additional fee to make the article OA. Again, to make the published version broadly accessible, the author does not have a Green OA option but must pay the fee for Gold OA.

In addition to the terminology of Gold and Green OA, it is useful to understand the Creative Commons (https://creativecommons.org/) acronyms and pictograms that are used to communicate both ownership and permitted uses of published content. These designations are increasingly used by publishers and are also referenced in the Sherpa Romeo database. The acronyms and their accompanying pictograms indicate what type of reuse of the content is permitted. The designations provide more information than the previously used copyright symbol (©), which simply conveyed that the author had certain rights – but did not specify what rights.

The Creative Commons license symbols always start with CC, as shown in Box 5.2, which illustrates the three types of licenses that are most common for work in political science and international relations. The first, CC BY, is the least restrictive. It allows others to use the work in a variety of ways, including commercial uses, as long as they give credit to the author. The second type of license, CC BY-NC, is similar to the CC BY license in that the work may be used and adapted in a variety of ways and must credit the author, but differs in that it permits only noncommercial uses. A third license, CC BY-NC-ND, is more restrictive and permits neither commercial uses nor adaptions or changes. Box 5.2 shows the pictograms for these three types of Creative Commons (CC) licenses (first column), defines the acronyms (second column), and explains the relationship between each pictogram element and two-letter acronym (third column). The CC licenses operate within the bounds of copyright law, but make it easier for reusers to understand what they are (not) permitted to do with a specific copyrighted work. They also make it easier for authors to indicate what uses of their work they permit.

BOX 5.2   CREATIVE COMMONS LICENSES

Pictogram	Definition	Explanation		
	CC BY:This license allows reusers to distribute, remix, adapt, and build upon the material in any medium or format, as long as attribution is given to the creator. The license allows for commercial use.	BY		= Credit must be given to the creator
	CC BY-NC: This license allows reusers to distribute, remix, adapt, and build upon the material in any medium or format for noncommercial purposes only, and only as long as attribution is given to the creator.	BY NC	 	= Credit must be given to the creator = Only noncommercial uses of the work are permitted
	CC BY-NC-ND: This license allows reusers to copy and distribute the material in any medium or format in unadapted form only, for noncommercial purposes only, and only as long as attribution is given to the creator.	BY NC ND	 	= Credit must be given to the creator = Only noncommercial uses of the work are permitted = No derivatives or adaptations of the work are permitted

Source: https://creativecommons.org/about/cclicenses/.

Although the CC licensing system does not straightforwardly translate to open access, the effort is related. Its explicit communication about the rights of authors and reusers is designed to encourage broader engagement with the products of scholarship. The Creative Commons webpages make clear that the non-profit organization's objective is to facilitate "universal access to research and education" in order to "drive a new era of development, growth, and productivity" (Creative Commons n.d.).

The different models of OA and the CC licensing system form an important new frontier in academic journal publishing. OA publishing looks attractive to university libraries that have faced increasing strains on their budgets, but the feasibility of these models is not yet proven. Depending on research agenda and location on the globe, some scholars may be able to reliably pay the costs of APCs out of their grants. However, it is unclear what proportion of scholarship in political science and international relations, globally, is grant-funded. Nor is it clear to what extent professional societies, foundations and universities will be able to help scholars defray the cost of APCs.

Interestingly, some searching in the DOAJ database suggests that most OA journals in political science and international relations currently do not charge APCs. Some of these are likely to be small journals that are – formally or informally – subsidized by the institution that employs its editor (Mehlum 2012). This option will not be available to journals that attract larger volumes of manuscripts (Gleditsch 2012). For the moment, OA publishing exists alongside the traditional subscription model, but its future is not fully clear. In the meantime, the move towards OA publishing has also spawned a darker industry of predatory publishing. This is the subject of the next section of this chapter.

5.3   OPEN ACCESS AND PREDATORY JOURNALS

As consumers of published research, scholars benefit from the accessibility of OA journals and OA articles in subscription-based journals. As producers of research, however, scholars seeking reputable, peer-reviewed outlets for their work now face a more complex publishing landscape. In addition to the traditional subscription-based and the newer OA journals, there are the so-called predatory journals. As the name suggests, such journals are best avoided.

Predatory journals can be quite difficult to identify. The producers of such journals often try very hard to make their publications' webpages look like those of reputable ones – at least to the untrained eye. What differentiates predatory journals from reputable ones is that the former are interested primarily in maximizing profit (Rich 2016). They often masquerade as OA journals and charge APCs. A closer look, however, reveals that careful investigation of such outlets is warranted.

First, predatory journals are usually not as forthcoming about their APCs as reputable ones. The information about such charges may be difficult to find. Scholars who are not aware that OA journals are funded through APCs may not realize that they should look for this information. Therefore, the bill comes as an unwelcome surprise that accompanies the news that the paper has been accepted for publication. At that point, it is more difficult to pull out – especially for those eager to finally see their work in print. However, a publication in a predatory journal will not do your scholarly reputation much good.

Second, predatory journals often claim to have a peer review process, but also promise to complete the review process in an unrealistically short period of time. Reputable journals try to expedite the process, but *none* can complete the process in ten days to two weeks. Predatory journals, on the other hand, frequently make very specific promises to complete the review process – and send you two reviews – in such a well-defined short period of time. Usually, articles are accepted after the first round of reviews. This rarely happens in reputable journals, as discussed in Chapter 2.

One scholar purposefully tried his luck at a predatory journal (Rich 2016). Instead of writing an article reporting on research, he simply copied song lyrics to create text the length of an article and sent it off. A few weeks later, he received an acceptance letter with two reviews – and a bill. This scholar sought to test the credibility of a predatory publication, which periodically sends emails soliciting manuscripts. Many predatory journals engage in this practice. Frequently, they simultaneously invite unsuspecting scholars to join the journal's editorial board. Be very careful about such offers.

Third, predatory journals are frequently quite broad in scope. On first glance, they may look like general journals, in the sense that they publish articles in all subfields of political science and international relations. Looking more closely, the statement of their scope and mission does not focus on contributions that are of interest to a broad range of scholars. Instead, the journal's aims imply that they "will publish anything and everything," as long as you pay the fee. Look at the scope and mission statements of the top journals in political science and international relations (as identified in, e.g., the JCR, see Chapter 1) and compare them to those of potentially predatory journals. If the latter seem overly inclusive of an extremely broad range of scholarship and lack an explanation of the criteria used to evaluate articles, investigate further.

Fourth, the webpages of predatory journals often look less professional than those of reputable journals (Rich 2016; Stop Predatory Journals n.d.). They may include problematic listings of editors and editorial board members. It may be worth checking the veracity of the information (Stop Predatory Journals n.d.). In sum, the webpages of predatory journals may provide some clues – but only if you know what to look for.

There are resources that can help scholars identify and avoid predatory journals, while maintaining the ability to take advantage of the possibilities provided by reputable OA ones. In Chapter 1, we discussed strategies for identifying journals. Those strategies work well for traditional subscription-based journals. Navigating the world of OA and predatory journals is more complicated – largely because it is populated with relatively new journals – but not impossible.

To investigate whether a specific journal is trustworthy, ask questions about the journal, its publisher, its editor(s) and editorial board, the review process, the costs associated with publishing your article, whether articles are indexed (and where), and whether the journal and its publisher are affiliated with any of the organizations that set standards for reputable OA journals. In the discussion that follows, we point to the resources offered by these industry initiatives. For easy reference, they are brought together in Box 5.3.

BOX 5.3 RESOURCES TO HELP DIFFERENTIATE REPUTABLE AND PREDATORY OA JOURNALS

Think, Check, Submit, https://thinkchecksubmit.org/.

Committee on Publication Ethics (COPE), https://publicationethics .org/.

Directory of Open Access Journals (DOAJ), https://doaj.org/.

Open Access Scholarly Publishers Association (OASPA), https:// oaspa.org/.

Stop Predatory Journals, https://predatoryjournals.com/.

INASP, https://www.inasp.info/project/journals-online-project.

First, if you have neither heard of the journal nor ever read any articles published in it, proceed with caution. Ask colleagues at your institution and others you know in the discipline. If they have not heard of the journal either, this could be a bad sign – but there are exceptions. For instance, *Political Research Exchange* (PRX), which we mentioned earlier in this chapter, was launched very recently (in 2019). It is an initiative of the European Consortium for Political Research (ECPR) and published by Taylor and Francis as a fully OA journal. The ECPR is a credible professional society and Taylor and Francis a reputable publisher of academic journals. Although members of the ECPR will have heard of this new journal through the society's communications, scholars in other parts of the world and who are not members of ECPR may not (yet) know about its existence.

That introduces the second issue: the journal's webpage should clearly identify the publication's publisher and contact information. Reputable publishers will identify themselves and often advertise their membership in various industry associations.

Third, check out the editor or editorial team, as well as the editorial board. Ask yourself – and your colleagues – whether you know anything about these scholars and their work. If you are unfamiliar with these scholars' names and work, this could indicate that you need to proceed with caution. A related strategy is to check the webpages and/ or curriculum vitae (CV) of the editor(s) and editorial board members to see if they mention their affiliation with the journal. Further, see if the information about the editor(s) and editorial board members is correct. If the listing for one is not, this may simply indicate a delay in updating the website. However, if there are a lot of inaccuracies *and* the scholars do not mention their affiliation with the journal on their website or CV, you have very likely stumbled upon evidence of a predatory journal.

Fourth, the review process should be explained clearly. Reputable journals will not promise that they will complete the review process in a very specific and short period of time – such as two weeks. Instead, they will use language that is somewhat vague (see Chapter 2).

Fifth, reputable OA journals will provide specific information about their APCs in an easy to find location on their website, as we discussed earlier in this chapter. Some predatory journals do provide information on APCs – sometimes under a slightly different name – but place this in a separate part of their website. Unless you are careful to investigate, you might miss this information – and receive a bill as a surprise along with an acceptance letter. This may be another sign that the journal is a predatory one.

Sixth, check the journal's webpage for any mention of the use of indexing services. This can usually be found with the basic information about the journal. Indexing services make your article findable, which is an important step in getting cited. Very likely, you have used them to identify at least some of the articles you cite in your own work. If the journal's webpage mentions no indexing services or only ones that you have not heard of and cannot identify, this could be a sign that the journal is not reputable.

Lastly, check whether the journal and its publisher are affiliated with organizations that set standards for the publishing industry. We have previously mentioned the Directory of Open Access Journals (DOAJ), a non-profit organization that has helped to establish best practices for OA publishing. DOAJ's directory includes journals that meet these standards. Hence, an OA journal listed in this directory is very likely to be reputable.

Both journals and their publishers can be members of the Committee on Publications Ethics (COPE 2020). This is also a non-profit organization. It provides, as the name suggests, guidance on ethical questions and best practices in publishing, as well as educational resources. Its website allows scholars to check whether specific journals are members of COPE and subscribe to its principles.

Publishers of OA journals may also be members of the Open Access Scholarly Publishers Association (OASPA 2020). Individual journals cannot be members, only publishing companies. Hence, it helps to be able to identify a journal's publisher. The OASPA's website spells out the criteria for membership, which include that the publisher must have at least one OA journal that is listed in the DOAJ and must be a member of COPE. The OASPA's website provides a listing of its members, which makes it easy for scholars to check the status of the publisher of a journal to which they consider submitting a paper.

Each of the above three organizations – DOAJ, COPE and OASPA – seek to foster transparency and trustworthiness in the (OA) publishing industry. A last source is INASP. Formerly known as the International Network for the Availability of Scientific Publications, INASP is now largely known just by its acronym. This non-profit organization seeks to improve the global visibility, as well as the quality, of scholarly journals published in the global South. In addition, it provides information about journals published in the global South through its Journals Online Project, which offers links to online platforms for journals published in several different countries and regions (see https://www.inasp.info/project/journals-online-project). Many are published online.

It may take some work to differentiate reputable OA journals from predatory ones. However, this new frontier in publishing also offers opportunities for the broader accessibility of research in political science and international relations. This is the subject of the next section of this chapter.

5.4   WHAT ARE THE BENEFITS AND COSTS OF PUBLISHING IN OPEN ACCESS JOURNALS?

The OA publishing landscape is a relatively recent phenomenon and presents uncertain terrain. It presents an inconsistent set of incentives. Scholars are both consumers and producers of published journal articles. Their interests across these roles diverge and their interests as scholars contain contradictory elements.

As consumers of others' research, scholars benefit from the wide accessibility of OA content. For scholars with less-than-optimal or no library access, the availability of OA content makes a broader range of work available. Indeed, a key argument in favor of OA has been greater accessibility, which is purported to level the playing field for scholars in the global South and others who do not have easy access to well-stocked research libraries (Nentwich 2008; Calise et al. 2010; Mehlum 2012; Atchison and Bull 2015; Jisc 2019).

A related argument in favor of OA is that, because it makes articles more accessible, it also results in more citations for authors. If so, this can be beneficial to scholars' careers. Two empirical studies in political science and international relations support the argument that the greater accessibility of OA content results in more citations (see Antelman 2004; Atchison and Bull 2015). These studies used content from subscription-based journals and compared articles that remained behind a paywall with those made Green OA, i.e., the authors had self-archived their articles on either a personal website or in an institutional repository. Both studies show that the Green OA articles had, on average, higher citation rates.

It is important to note that both studies compared content from prestigious journals in the discipline. In other words, the perceived merits of the journal were held constant as the studies compared OA and behind-paywall content. It is unclear whether this finding can be generalized to argue that content from fully OA publications will also be cited more extensively than content from traditional subscription-based journals. Accessibility of research may well play a role in the frequency of citation, but the perceived quality of the article matters as well. Quite often, scholars use the journal in which an article is published as an indicator of its quality. As yet, there are relatively few fully OA journals in political science and international relations. The ones that do exist are relatively new. It will take some time for these journals to build reputations for publishing high-quality scholarship. Hence, the available data may appear to support the conclusion that OA leads to more citations, but they did not compare traditional subscription-based journals and OA journals.

The lure of more citations may persuade some scholars to publish their articles OA. After all, the discipline – and academia more generally – increasingly focuses on such metrics. The importance of citation counts as a measure of a scholar's impact – and associated professional benefits – may well be a powerful argument in favor of OA publishing. To be sure, we do not argue that citation counts and associated metrics are the "best" way to evaluate a scholar's impact; we only claim that these measures are widely used as such and that this is likely to influence the behavior of scholars who perceive a need to enhance their citation counts.

That said, Gold OA is not free and most publishers place important constraints on Green OA. Scholars attracted to the promise of additional citations will face the prospect of paying for the APCs associated with OA. This is not yet a substantial impediment as many journals listed in the DOAJ do not charge APCs at this time. Some are currently funded by grants or supported by a professional society. In other instances, however, professional societies rely on income from the journals they sponsor. Commercial journal publishers may be willing to invest in the start-up of a new OA journal, but will ultimately seek a return on their investment and make a profit. As Gleditsch (2012: 214) has noted, journals are a commercial product and revenue "has to come from author fees, either for submission, for publication, or both. This can be a significant impediment for some authors, and where funding is available it is likely ... to come from the same public and foundation sources that fund library subscriptions."

Hence, scholars may broadly benefit from the accessibility of OA publishing in their role as *consumers* of research publications and in terms of the prestige associated with additional citations – if the evidence regarding the latter is indeed generalizable. However, as *producers* of research, scholars may face difficulties they did not encounter previously. As journals published by commercial publishers inevitably start demanding payment of APCs, scholars will need to identify funding sources to help defray the cost. For some, it may be possible to build this into a grant – although the ability to secure grant funding is unevenly distributed, both across the globe and across research agendas. Others may be able to appeal to funds made available for this purpose at their university. However, limited funds that currently exist for this purpose at universities in the USA have restrictions. Most importantly, there is frequently a maximum amount any individual researcher can access per year. Depending on the specific ceiling that an employing institution has set, this could constrain a scholar's ability to be productive. Further, the ability of universities to support the costs of the APCs their faculty's scholarly work incurs will be just as unevenly distributed across institutions and geographic locations as their ability to support the cost of conventional library holdings – well-endowed universities are likely to provide more liberal support than poorly endowed ones. And while publishers may continue to provide discounts on – or waive altogether – the APCs for scholars from the global South, it is unclear whether this will level the global playing field.

In sum, scholars may benefit from the easier access to published work and the enhanced citation counts, but may face new problems in their ability to publish. Rather than rejoicing over the notification that their work has been accepted by a high-quality journal, scholars may in the future face the agonizing question of how they will pay the bill for the APCs. As a new frontier in academic publishing, the implications of OA have not yet fully come into focus. That said, OA will have important consequences for both scholars and the publishing industry.

6. Maximizing the impact of your scholarship

In this chapter, we will discuss strategies on how to increase the impact of the scholar's published work. One way to learn about impactful scholarship is to actively engage in the review process by becoming a reviewer for journals. The remainder of this chapter will discuss strategies to increase the impact of the scholar's published articles.

6.1 LEARNING ABOUT PUBLISHING BY DOING REVIEWS

It may at first glance seem odd to discuss active engagement as a reviewer in a chapter devoted to maximizing the impact of your own scholarship. However, there is a lot to be learnt from reading other scholars' work, both in its published form and as anonymous manuscripts during the review process. Scholars reading this book will have had ample opportunity to read published scholarship in political science and international relations, as well as in their specific area of inquiry. Serving as a reviewer requires a different kind of examination of a manuscript than reading published work.

As a reviewer, your role is to analyze a paper for strengths and weaknesses, and to suggest ways in which it can be improved. Engaging in this process as a reviewer will also sharpen the skills needed to dissect your own manuscripts. As a reviewer, you may get irritated at a manuscript that takes a slow and winding path to reveal its key research question, which you finally discover on page seven. If so, take the time not only to suggest in your review that the author might have revealed the research question sooner, but also make a mental note to ensure that you check whether your own work gets to the point quickly. Reviewing manuscripts is an opportunity to consider why an introduction is (in)effective, why a specific way of framing an argument is (not) persuasive, and what does (not) make writing clear and easy to read. Hence, reviewing presents an opportunity to learn about effective writing in the format you will be using most: the peer-reviewed journal article (Miller et al. 2013).

Many journals will share the decision as well as the other reviews for the manuscript with the reviewers. Hence, participating in the review process allows you to gain comparative perspective into your own insights into the manuscript you reviewed, but also helps to see how different scholars vary in their interpretation of the same text (Miller et al. 2013). Ask yourself: what might the manuscript's author have done differently to minimize such differences? Consider how such insights can help to improve your own writing. Finally, there is some evidence that reviewing results in a modest improvement in the likelihood of getting published (Breuning et al. 2018).

That raises the question: how do you become a reviewer for academic journals in political science and international relations? Despite claims by senior scholars that they are overburdened with review requests and editors' claims that it is difficult to find reviewers, there are many scholars who are rarely (or never) asked (Djupe 2015; Publons 2018; Wilkinson 2020). Those who are asked to review also hail disproportionally from the USA, even though manuscripts are submitted by an increasingly global array of scholars (Publons 2018).

One possibility is to register your name and areas of expertise in the journal's reviewer database. It is not difficult to register yourself, so it is a low-cost way to increase your odds of being identified as a potential reviewer. This does not guarantee that you will be asked, but editors do search their journal's reviewer database, using keywords, to identify appropriate reviewers. Some evidence of this practice can be gleaned from a study that reported that 40.6 percent of reviewers were first identified by an editor after they submitted a manuscript (Publons 2018). Most often, scholars first register their name in a journal's database when they submit a manuscript, hence the connection between the submission and review request.

In addition to using the journal's database, editors and editorial assistants at well-established and prestigious journals also spend time combing through conference programs, paper archives and so on, to identify potential reviewers. Editors at smaller journals with little or no staff have less time to invest in such searches, which makes it worthwhile to register in their reviewer database. This is likely to have a better payoff for those with the PhD in hand. Although some journals will include advanced graduate students in their reviewer pool, others will only seek out scholars who have earned their PhD.

Although professional benefits can be derived from serving as a reviewer, many scholars are initially unsure what is expected of them in that role. Most graduate programs do not include training in how to write reviews, nor do they systematically teach any of the other aspects of service as a reviewer for an academic journal. Providing such training is beyond the scope of this book, but in Box 6.1 we list two online courses and other resources to increase your knowledge about the review process and instill confidence in your abilities as a reviewer.

BOX 6.1   LEARNING ABOUT PEER REVIEW

For free online training in peer reviewing:

1. Publons: Learn to Peer Review with Confidence (offers actual review experience and feedback). Available at https://publons .com/community/academy/.
2. Elsevier, certified peer reviewer course; offers certificate. Available at https://researcheracademy.elsevier.com/navigating -peer-review/certified-peer-reviewer-course/introduction -certified-peer-reviewer-course.

Useful written guidance is provided in:

1. Beth Miller, Jon Pevehouse, Ron Rogowski, Dustin Tingley and Rick Wilson (2013), "How to Be a Peer Reviewer: A Guide for Recent and Soon-to-Be PhDs," PS: Political Science and Politics 46(1): 120–23.
2. Committee on Publication Ethics (COPE) (2019), "Ethical Guidelines for Peer Reviewers," https://doi.org/10.24318/cope .2019.1.9 (guide also available in Chinese and Spanish).

Some publishers also provide online guidance and tutorials:

1. Cambridge University Press; https://www.cambridge.org/core/ services/aop-file-manager/file/5a1eb62e67f405260662a0df/ Refreshed-Guide-Peer-Review-Journal.pdf.
2. Taylor and Francis; https://editorresources.taylorandfrancis.com/ reviewer-guidelines/.
3. Sage; https://us.sagepub.com/sites/default/files/how_to_become _a_reviewer.pdf.
4. Springer; https://www.springer.com/gp/authors-editors/authora ndreviewertutorials/howtopeerreview/how-to-peer-review/ 10285380.
5. Wiley; https://authorservices.wiley.com/Reviewers/journal -reviewers/index.html.

6.2   PROMOTING YOUR PUBLISHED WORK

In the not too distant past, most academics did not think about promoting their work. Indeed, many academics still squirm uncomfortably at the notion. However, the rise of various forms of electronic communication has changed the scholarly landscape in significant ways. There are new ways to create visibility for scholarship in political science and international relations, both within the academy and beyond. Here, we discuss strategies to share your research and offer some reasons why it can be useful to pursue these paths.

First, research articles tend to be written to share research findings with other scholars in the field. Scholars have traditionally assumed that others will automatically find, read and cite their work once it is available on "first view" or in print. The evidence – most notably on citations – suggests otherwise. Although King's claim that the "modal number of citations to articles in political science is zero" may overstate the case, there is great variation in the degree to which articles get noticed (King 1995: 445; see also Samuels 2011).

The pattern of citations suggests that this variation cannot simply be attributed to the merits of a given article. Consider, for instance, evidence that articles authored by women tend to get cited less than those written by men (Maliniak et al. 2013; Mitchell et al. 2013). It is unknown whether there are similar inequalities in the citation patterns of the scholarship produced by other underrepresented groups, such as persons of color or LGBTQ scholars – there is a dearth of research on the subject. However, the available information suggests that citation patterns are not simply a function of the merits of the scholarly contribution of an article. Hence, scholars may benefit from taking a more active role in ensuring that their work is noticed and integrated into subsequent work.

There are several strategies available to promote your work. Some journals now offer "video abstracts." These are short videos in which the author summarizes the article. Sometimes these videos take the format of a brief interview with the editor. If you have an opportunity to tape a video abstract, think carefully about how to present the core of the paper's argument concisely and without resorting to a lot of jargon. This can make it attractive to a broader audience. The video abstract will appear on the journal's webpage, alongside the link to the full article. Of course, this presumes that other scholars will access the journal's webpage and take the time to view the videos.

There are more direct strategies to let others know about your new and forthcoming work. Increasingly, scholars seek to draw attention to their work by posting a link to their newest article on their Facebook page or Twitter feed, including also posting to groups in which they have membership. Depending on the size of your network on these social media outlets, this can help others learn about your work. To some, it feels awkward to "advertise" in this way. The key is to find a strategy for sharing information about new work without sounding like a crass salesperson. Some scholars have used self-deprecating humor, but there are many ways to convey enthusiasm about your publication that avoids an off-putting in-your-face quality. Find a way that feels right to you to get your work noticed by other scholars whose research agendas intersect with yours – and realize that you are offering them a shortcut to finding out about interesting new scholarship.

Second, there are new ways to communicate your research to general audiences. Publishing about your work in venues directed at such audiences may also net additional academic readers – and may have other spinoffs as well. Consider the story Stephen Dyson (2015) tells in the preface to his book *Otherworldly Politics*. He writes that two essays he published in the *Washington Post*'s blog The Monkey Cage led the editor of a publishing house to approach him about writing a book. Dyson's blog posts were not derived from his scholarship but led to a book contract. That may be rather rare, but it suggests that scholars and publishers are among the general public that reads online publications.

Of course, writing for a general audience is different from writing for an academic journal. It requires a different way of thinking and writing, one that is more akin to conversations in the classroom. A general audience is not interested in a literature review or detailed theory, and may not care about the reasons for using a specific statistical technique. Instead, such a readership will be more interested in the findings and implications of the research.

Developing the skill to write informative and engaging articles that are based on solid research but intended for a general audience may take some effort. Start by reading the online publications you might consider targeting to see how published pieces present research findings. The ability to reach out to a general audience by publishing short online articles not only expands the impact of your scholarly contributions – it also offers opportunities to make new connections (Montgomery 2017). Increasingly, universities value scholars who develop a "public profile," which includes various forms of engagement with audiences beyond the walls of the academy. For universities, public engagement by their faculty demonstrates that the institution produces useful knowledge and thus helps in the institution's communications with funders and legislators.

Whereas in the past most academic research that reached a general audience was written by journalists who would "translate" the scientific work to something the general public could understand, there are now new opportunities for scholars to write for a general audience themselves (Montgomery 2017). Above, we mentioned The Monkey Cage, one of several blogs sponsored by the *Washington Post*. Another online publication that seeks contributions from academics is The Conversation, which has editions in different countries and languages. Box 6.2 provides links to these online publications' webpages with information on what they publish and how you can connect with them. The box also includes links to two additional sources that seek to connect scholars with general audiences (and policymakers).

BOX 6.2 WRITING FOR GENERAL AUDIENCES

Bridging the Gap: Connecting Research and Policy.
  http://bridgingthegapproject.org/.

The Conversation.
  https://theconversation.com/us/pitches.

The Monkey Cage.
  https://www.washingtonpost.com/politics/2019/06/10/about
  -monkey-cage/.

The OpEd Project.
  https://www.theopedproject.org/.

Online publications are most interested in contributions from political scientists when they can make a connection with the news or with current issues more broadly conceived. These publications will look for proven expertise, as well as an interesting angle on the subject. Some will work with you to develop an appealing or thought-provoking way to frame the piece. Other publications leave it to you to come up with a way to connect your research to current news.

Expertise is most easily established with reference to published work, but it is possible to publish a piece online that is derived from current research that has not yet been published. In the latter case, the brief online article may generate interest in the current research and your expertise. A potential downside is that publishing an online article ahead of submitting the related scholarly manuscript to a journal can make it more difficult to maintain the double-blind nature of the review process. Potential reviewers may have seen the online publication. As long as such reviewers pledge to offer a fair and impartial evaluation, editors tend to permit such deviations from the double-blind review principle. In other words, this potential downside should not be an impediment to publishing online when you can offer evidence that speaks to a current issue.

In cases where the online publication derives from published work, it may be possible to have the academic article made accessible to the readers of the online publication for a brief window of time. Academic journal publishers refer to this as "ungating" the article, i.e., removing the barrier represented by the need for a subscription to the journal in order to access the article. Publishers ungate articles to generate visibility for both the article and the journal, and to enhance the metrics of the publication's impact – measured as the number of downloads of the article.

In sum, there are multiple strategies to pursue additional visibility for your research. At any given time, some of these will make more sense for your research than others. In addition, new opportunities for promoting your research will emerge as new types of media are developed. The bottom line is that it makes sense to expend some effort on enhancing the visibility of your scholarship by sharing it with colleagues in political science and international relations, and with broader general audiences.

6.3   GETTING READ VERSUS GETTING CITED

Publication is in part about sharing research findings with the scholarly community. Most scholars appreciate knowing that others read their work, find it interesting, and build on it in their own work. This is how a field of study moves forward in building an increasingly sophisticated understanding of the phenomena being studied. One key mechanism through which scholars discover that their articles have an impact is to see them cited by other scholars. We discuss the merits of counting citations, as well as various ways in which citations are measured, and then pivot to some alternative ways to think about impact.

Citations are easy to count and have become a standard way of asserting the merits of specific articles and a scholar's overall body of work. However, citation and merit are not the same thing. Although highly cited articles are often thought-provoking, some less well-cited articles offer equally meritorious content.

Why are some articles widely cited and, more importantly, why is other good scholarship sometimes overlooked? Consider that there are hundreds of journals in political science and international relations. A low estimate is the 225 journals for which the *Journal Citation Reports* (JCR) calculates an Impact Factor (IF). There is variation in the number of issues published annually, but the modal number is four. The number of articles published per issue varies as well, but let's assume a low average of six articles. Simple math suggests that one journal publishes, on average, $6 \times 4 = 24$ articles annually. Multiplying that by the 225 journals results in 5,400 new articles published in political science and international relations each year!

Remember that this is a low estimate. There are many more journals than those tracked by the JCR. Also, many journals publish more than six articles per issue and some have more than four issues per year. That said, most scholars will read only articles that relate to their own research and teaching interests. Hence, scholars who try to read every new article that is related to their own research area would read only a fraction of the total number of articles published in the discipline's journals overall. However, this would still add to a substantial number of new articles and scholars fill their days with more than reading others' work: they teach, conduct research and write their own articles, among other tasks. Most develop strategies for identifying those new articles that are most relevant for them to read.

In some cases, scholars will have some insight into forthcoming work because they have seen the research presented at a conference or have reviewed manuscripts for journals. Many also get alerts from journals to which they subscribe (often as part of their membership in a professional association) about articles that are newly published on "early view," as well as the tables of contents of each new issue. These strategies are useful, given the high volume of new articles published, but the result is that scholars tend to be more likely to notice articles that are published in the journals with which they are most familiar, unless interesting articles in other publications have been pointed out to them by others in their network. In other words, scholars become aware of one another's work – a first step to deciding to read and cite it – through a process that is social and political (Jensenius et al. 2018). This process is very often structured by membership in professional societies. Such societies frequently sponsor journals that scholars receive as part of their membership. Many scholars find participation in professional societies fruitful. However, this can also create networks through which information flows that are not neutral and may overlook or exclude certain groups, which results in their work being noticed – and cited – less often (Jensenius et al. 2018).

The patterns of citation are not only a function of scholarly networks, however. Research on the pattern of citations of scholarship by women and men has shown that, on average, women tend to get cited less often than men (Maliniak et al. 2013; Mitchell et al. 2013). There is less tangible evidence of other inequities in citation patterns, because there has been less empirical research in areas other than gender. Another issue is that the accumulation of citations is facilitated when there are many other scholars working in a specific area of inquiry. Conversely, in research communities that are relatively smaller, there will also be fewer other scholars to cite your work (Jensenius et al. 2018). And it takes time to build a record of citations. Scholars in the earlier stages of their careers will have lower citation counts than those who have spent more years in the profession. The latter have not only had more years to be active in the profession, but others have had time to read and cite their work. Although some articles accumulate citations quickly (and may subsequently be largely forgotten), other articles catch on quite slowly with few citations in the first few years after publication but garner increasing interest over time. The latter is especially likely in the case of articles containing highly innovative ideas, which may take time to be discovered and valued by others (Jensenius et al. 2018).

Taken together, the accumulation of citations to a scholar's articles is determined by multiple factors. Promoting your work may help, but it is not the only factor that influences how quickly citations accumulate. After delving a bit more into metrics associated with citations, we will discuss alternative perspectives on the impact of scholarship.

The conventional way to think about impact is to consider the total number of citations to the body of work produced by a specific scholar. The total number of times a scholar's articles (and books) are cited conveys something about the centrality of that person's collective body of work to other scholars in political science and international relations. However, it reveals rather little about the pattern of citations – is the scholar widely cited because she has produced quite a lot of articles or is there one ground-breaking publication that has attracted a lot of attention? The same overall number of citations can be the result of these very different patterns. The *h*-index was created to simultaneously account for the *productivity* of a scholar – measured as the overall number of articles published – and the *impact* of her work – measured as the number of times each article has been cited. It is easy to determine the *h*-index by arranging your publications from most cited to least cited and finding the cutoff point where article *h* has been cited at least *h* times.

Consider the example in Box 6.3, which shows two fictitious scholars who have published ten articles and accumulated one hundred citations each. Their achievements are similar both in terms of the number of articles and the number of citations. However, their *h*-index differs, because the citations are distributed differently among the articles they each have published. The citations to Scholar 1's work are concentrated on the two highest cited articles, whereas Scholar 2's citations have a flatter distribution. Scholar 1 has an *h*-index of 5, because there are five articles with at least five citations. Scholar 2 fares better with an *h*-index of 7, because there are seven articles with at least seven citations. Although the overall number of citations of both scholars is exactly the same (one hundred), the distribution of citations affects the *h*-index. It rewards the slow-and-steady scholar who produces many articles that all garner at least a moderate amount of citations over the one with a few highly cited articles.

An alternative to the *h*-index, the *g*-index, adjusts the formula to take into account the average number of citations, which means that a scholar's highly cited articles compensate for lower-cited ones. Despite the differences in the number of citations for specific articles, both fictitious scholars in the example from Box 6.3 have one hundred citations and ten articles, resulting in a *g*-index of 10 for each. Neither the *h*-index nor the *g*-index do very well at recognizing the impact of a scholar who has published one or two ground-breaking articles and not much else, which led Harzing (2020) to conclude that such a scholar is better off focusing on the total number of citations. In sum, the *h*-index and the *g*-index measure impact in slightly different ways, but both reward scholars for building a consistent record of publication over time.

BOX 6.3 EXAMPLES OF H-INDEX

Number of articles	Scholar 1	Scholar 2
1	30	20
2	25	20
3	15	15
4	10	13
5	7 – cutoff: h = 5	12
6	5	10
7	4	8 – cutoff: h = 7
8	3	2
9	1	0
10	0	0
Total citations	*100*	*100*

There are several databases that track citations to articles produced by individual scholars, but they do not all provide the same information. Some are freely available, but others require a subscription. First, the Social Science Citation Index (SSCI) is part of the same company that produces the JCR (Web of Science/Clarivate). Scholars usually access it through their university library – if it has a subscription. The libraries of research universities in the USA often subscribe, but others may not. The SSCI provides an h-index score, as well as the total number of times the scholar's work was cited and the number of articles in which those citations were found.

Second, Scopus is published by Elsevier, the same company that also created Scimago to measure journal impact. Scholars can access Scopus free of charge at https://www.scopus.com/, to see their h-index and the number of articles on which the calculation is based. However, the site does not indicate the number of citations per article, the overall number of citations, or other information used to calculate the h-index.

Third, Google Scholar is also freely accessible and provides a lot of detail. Scholars can view the total number of citations and their h-index, as well as an $i10$-index, which indicates the number of articles that have garnered at least ten citations. In addition to the total count, Google Scholar shows the same measures for the last five years. The two fictitious scholars in Box 6.3 fare differently with regard to the $i10$-index, just as they did with the *h*-index. Scholar 1 has four articles with at least ten citations and therefore has accumulated an *i*10-index of 4, whereas Scholar 2 has six articles with at least ten citations and an *i*10-index of 6. Once again, a consistent record of publications, with each article receiving a moderate number of citations, is rewarded.

In addition to the metrics described in the previous paragraph, Google Scholar also makes the list of publications and the number of citations each article has received accessible. It is possible to check through the list and make sure it is accurate. It is also possible to add articles that are missing and eliminate ones that are not yours – Google Scholar occasionally includes articles written by a scholar with the same family name and initial, who may work in an entirely different discipline.

Google Scholar is quite widely used because it is easily accessible – anyone who can get online can find it. Comparing the metrics offered by Google Scholar with those of Scopus and the SSCI will show different results for the same scholar. This is due to differences in the range of publications that each examines to count the number of articles and associated citations for each scholar in their database. Generally, the reported *h*-index and overall number of citations are highest in Google Scholar and lowest in the SSCI, with Scopus falling in between.

Despite the shortcomings of these indices, they are widely used as a metric by which to judge the relative impact of scholars. In political science and international relations, the *h*-index is popular along with the total number of citations a scholar's body of work has accumulated. However, not all scholarship is equally likely to attract a lot of citations. Some articles are much more widely read than cited. This is especially true for the scholarship of teaching and learning (SoTL) and the sociology of the discipline.

The latter are articles that examine various aspects of political science and international relations, such as Maliniak et al. (2013), Mitchell et al. (2013), Breuning et al. (2015; 2018), and Jensenius et al. (2018) – all cited earlier. Scholars often read these articles with great interest and discuss their findings with colleagues. However, unless they themselves undertake a similar type of study, they will not have much occasion to cite these articles in their own work. Scholars who write articles examining the discipline know that these articles will not be widely cited, but anticipate a different type of impact. For instance, as a consequence of research that has shown repeatedly that women tend to be cited less than men, some journal editors now ask authors to make sure to check through their reference list and consider whether they can make it more gender-balanced.

The scholarship of teaching and learning (SoTL) examines various aspects of pedagogy and curriculum. In political science and international relations, such work is found primarily in the *Journal of Political Science Education, International Studies Perspectives* and *PS: Political Science and Politics*. Articles on teaching techniques – such as in-class exercises or simulations – are well-read, because instructors often look for ways to improve upon their teaching strategies. Articles examining the effectiveness of various pedagogical techniques are also well-read, because they give instructors insight into the merits of various teaching strategies. However, only a fraction of the consumers of this information is active as a scholar in this area. Hence, SoTL articles are far more widely read than cited.

Before the existence of the Internet, the impact of SoTL and the sociology of the discipline were very difficult to measure. Many of the conversations sparked by this work would have taken place in offices and hallways, or during informal interactions at professional meetings. That is probably still the case, but the Internet has made it possible to capture those interactions that occur online. This is the province of Altmetrics, which we also mentioned in Chapter 1. Research shows that it captures a different type of impact than is measured by more traditional indicators of scholarly impact (Costas et al. 2015; Williams 2017).

Altmetrics gathers data on the usage of articles from social media, traditional media and online reference managers (e.g., Mendeley). It then categorizes this data in various ways. The most familiar is the colorful "donut," which provides "information on the types and the amount of attention the research output has received" (Williams 2017: 313; see also https://www.altmetric.com/about-our-data/the-donut-and-score/). Each color in the donut indicates a different type of attention. For example, the donut might indicate that the article was mentioned by fifteen tweeters (light blue), one person on Facebook (bright blue), one blog (yellow), read by twenty-two on Mendeley (dark red), and mentioned once in Wikipedia (gray). The more different types of attention an article has gathered, the more colorful the donut. Altmetrics further captures the geographic location where the online mentions originate, thus allowing insight into global spread of ideas.

The information gathered and disseminated by Altmetrics makes it possible to demonstrate new and different types of impact in a way that is comparable to the traditional impact through citation by other scholars.

It provides scholars with tangible counts of mentions on various types of online platforms that they can use to show that their articles have had a "real world" impact (Williams 2017).

Publishers often also track the number of views and downloads of articles – something that has become possible now that journals are most often accessed online rather than as paper copies on library shelves. Views and downloads demonstrate interest in specific articles in a more immediate way than citations, which take a longer time to accumulate. Views and downloads are also important for articles that are less likely to garner many citations, such as SoTL articles and the sociology of the discipline. Hence, views and downloads provide another complement to the traditional measures of impact through citations.

In sum, the metrics used to evaluate the impact of scholars and their work play an important role in political science and international relations. It is important to understand both their value and their limitations. In addition to metrics focused on citation by other scholars, there are now metrics that evaluate other types of interest and impact. In evaluating the progress of your career, consider these various metrics in combination to obtain a more holistic view of the impact of your work.

6.4   CONSISTENT PRODUCTIVITY AND IMPACT

Getting published in the best journals in political science and international relations requires persistence. It also requires the ability to work on multiple projects simultaneously – or rather, to have multiple projects at various stages of completion at any one point in time. As we described in Chapter 1, after submitting one manuscript you have time to work on one or more others. Dividing your time between multiple projects also helps to attenuate the downside of the publishing process – the rejection letters that you will inevitably receive. A disappointment regarding one project is less devastating when work on another is progressing well.

Although not every manuscript may be accepted by the journal in which you would prefer to have it published, every manuscript can find a "home." Many scholars in political science and international relations have been told to always send their articles to one of the top journals first. That is not always good advice. It is often wiser to spend some time weighing the fit between the manuscript and the journal, identifying several suitable outlets, and sending the paper to one that appears to be a good fit (as we discussed in Chapter 1). Your best assessment of fit does not guarantee that the manuscript will receive an invitation to revise and resubmit, but it is far more likely that the paper will find a home with fewer attempts than if you send it to the most prestigious journal first and go down the line from there. Remember that every additional attempt adds time to the overall process of getting a paper published.

Of course, judging fit is a skill just like every other aspect of publishing your scholarly work. Although scholars improve their ability to judge the fit of their manuscripts as they become more experienced with the publishing process, we do not know any scholars whose experience allows them to avoid receiving rejection letters from journals altogether. Rejections remain part of the process even for well-established scholars. No one likes this, but most of us learn to pick ourselves up and keep going. Persistence pays.

In your efforts to find suitable outlets for your research, it may pay to look beyond the boundaries of political science and international relations to interdisciplinary journals. Such journals are not a good option for manuscripts that fit squarely within the scope of research questions addressed within the discipline or one of its subfields. However, manuscripts that draw on an adjacent discipline may be a great fit for such a journal. Consider, for instance, scholarship that integrates knowledge from political science and psychology, sociology, economics or communication, or work that intersects with the study of specific geographic regions of the world, or that focuses on a problem studied across different disciplines. As with journals in political science, carefully examine the aims of the interdisciplinary journal as well as the contents of some recent issues. This will help to evaluate whether the journal might be open to the kind of work represented by your manuscript. In addition, it may be useful to get advice from colleagues about the value of publishing in interdisciplinary journals. Some academic departments will welcome such publications, whereas others prefer that scholars stay within their disciplinary boundaries. Knowing whether interdisciplinary publications are valued will help you determine whether or not to consider submitting your manuscript to such an outlet.

Publishing in the best journals is ultimately about gaining insight into the kind of work that various journals tend to favor and submitting your manuscripts to those outlets where it will have better odds. Most scholars do not consistently produce the kinds of manuscripts that fare well at the most prestigious journals. However, almost all endeavor to produce at least some work that will have a good chance of being published in a top journal. If your first article does not land in a top journal, do not give up.

A subsequent manuscript may. Strive to make each paper better than the last one and to make your work as good as the papers published in the best journals.

Realize also that the metrics by which the discipline judges a scholar's body of work favor consistency over time. Scholars who produce more articles that are all moderately cited will not only accumulate a large number of citations, but also a very respectable *h*-index score. This is true not only for scholars who have published in the most prestigious journals, but for all scholars who have published in outlets that reach an audience of a reasonable size. Scholarly careers depend on consistently filling and emptying the pipeline of manuscripts over time, not on one smash hit.

References

Albert, Tim, and Elizabeth Wager. 2003. "How to Handle Authorship Disputes: A Guide for New Researchers." COPE (Committee on Publication Ethics). https://publicationethics.org/resources/guidelines-new/how-handle -authorship-disputesa-guide-new-researchers. Accessed September 30, 2020.

American Economic Association [AEA]. 2020. "JEL Classification Codes Guide." www.aeaweb.org/jel/guide/jel.php.

Anderson, Richard G. 2013. "Registration and Replication: A Comment." *Political Analysis* 21(1): 38–9.

Antelman, Kristin. 2004. "Do Open-Access Articles Have a Greater Research Impact?" *College & Research Libraries* 65(5): 372–82.

Atchison, Amy, and Jonathan Bull. 2015. "Will Open Access Get Me Cited? An Analysis of the Efficacy of Open Access Publishing in Political Science." *PS: Political Science & Politics* 48(1): 129–37.

Belcher, Wendy Laura. 2019. *Writing Your Journal Article in Twelve Weeks: A Guide to Academic Publishing Success*, 2nd ed. Chicago: University of Chicago Press.

Bhattacharjee, Yudhijit. 2013. "The Mind of a Con Man." *New York Times Magazine*, April 26. https://www.nytimes.com/2013/04/28/magazine/diederik -stapels-audacious-academic-fraud.html#:~:text=Diederik%20Stapel%2C %20a%20Dutch%20social%20psychologist%2C%20perpetrated%20an ,nature.%20Koos%20Breukel%20for%20The%20New%20York%20Times. Accessed October 15, 2020.

Bhattacharya, Srobana. 2014. "Institutional Review Board and International Field Research in Conflict Zones." *PS: Political Science & Politics* 47(4): 840–44.

Biggs, Jeffrey. 2008. "Allocating the Credit in Collaborative Research." *PS: Political Science & Politics* 41(1): 246–7.

Boyer, Mark. 2003. "Symposium on Replication in International Studies Research." *International Studies Perspectives* 4: 72–107.

Breuning, Marijke, Jeremy Backstrom, Jeremy Brannon, Ben Gross, and Michael Widmeier. 2015. "Reviewer Fatigue? Why Scholars Decline to Review their Peers' Work." *PS: Political Science and Politics* 48(4): 595–600.

Breuning, Marijke, Benjamin Isaak Gross, Ayal Feinberg, Melissa Martinez, Ramesh Sharma, and John Ishiyama. 2018. "Clearing the Pipeline? Gender and the Review Process at the APSR." *PS: Political Science and Politics* 51(3): 629–34.

Calise, Mauro, Rosanna de Rosa, and Xavier Fernández i Marín. 2010. "Electronic Publishing, Knowledge Sharing and Open Access: A New Environment for Political Science." *European Political Science* 9(S): 50–60.

Carey, Benedict. 2015. "Study on Attitudes Toward Same-Sex Marriage Is Retracted by a Scientific Journal." *New York Times*. https://www.nytimes .com/2015/05/29/science/journal-science-retracts-study-on-gay-canvassers -and-same-sex-marriage.html. Accessed October 12, 2020.

Carsey, Thomas. 2014. "Making DA-RT a Reality". *PS: Political Science & Politics* 47 (1): 72–7.

CDC [Centers for Disease Control and Prevention]. 2020. U.S. *Public Health Service Syphilis Study at Tuskegee*. https://www.cdc.gov/tuskegee/timeline .htm. Accessed October 21, 2020.

COPE [Committee on Publication Ethics]. 2019. "Ethical Guidelines for Peer Reviewers." https://doi.org/10.24318/cope.2019.1.9. Accessed May 20, 2020. (Also available in Chinese and Spanish.)

COPE [Committee on Publication Ethics]. 2020. https://publicationethics.org/. Accessed June 8, 2020.

Costas, Rodrigo, Zohreh Zahedi, and Paul Wouters. 2015. "Do Altmetrics Correlate with Citations? Extensive Comparison of Almetric Indicators with Citations from a Multidisciplinary Perspective." *Journal of the Association for Information Science and Technology* 66(10): 2003–19.

Craig, Iain D., Liz Ferguson, and Adam T. Finch. 2014. "Journals Ranking and Impact Factors: How the Performance of Journals is Measured," in Bill Cope and Angus Phillips (eds.), *The Future of the Academic Journal*, 2nd ed., Amsterdam: Elsevier/Chandos Publishing, pp. 259–98.

Creative Commons. n.d. "Program Areas." https://creativecommons.org/about/ program-areas/. Accessed June 5, 2020.

Cronin-Furman, Kate, and Milli Lake. 2018. "Ethics Abroad: Fieldwork in Fragile and Violent Contexts." *PS: Political Science & Politics* 51(3): 607–14.

Dafoe, Allan. 2014. "Science Deserves Better: The Imperative to Share Complete Replication Files." *PS: Political Science & Politics* 47(1): 60–66.

Desposato, Scott (ed.). 2016. *Ethics and Experiments: Problems and Solutions for Social Scientists and Policy Professionals*. New York: Routledge.

Desposato, Scott. 2016a. "Introduction," in Scott Desposato (ed.), *Ethics and Experiments: Problems and Solutions for Social Scientists and Policy Professionals*, New York: Routledge, pp. 1–22.

Desposato, Scott. 2016b. "Conclusion and Recommendations," in Scott Desposato (ed.), *Ethics and Experiments: Problems and Solutions for Social Scientists and Policy Professionals*, New York: Routledge, pp. 267–89.

Directory of Open Access Journals [DOAJ]. 2020. https://doaj.org. Accessed June 4, 2020.

Djupe, Paul A. 2015. "Peer Reviewing in Political Science: New Survey Results." *PS: Political Science and Politics* 48(2): 346–51.

Dyson, Stephen Benedict. 2015. *Otherworldly Politics: The International Relations of Star Trek, Game of Thrones, and Battlestar Galactica*. Baltimore, MD: Johns Hopkins University Press.

Elman, Colin, Diana Kapiszewski, Andrew Moravcsik, and Sebastian Karcher. 2017. "A Guide to Annotation for Transparent Inquiry (ATI)." https://qdr.syr .edu/ati/guide-ati. Accessed May 11, 2021.

Fisher, Bonnie S., Craig T. Cobane, Thomas M. Vander Ven, and Francis T. Cullen. 1998. "How Many Authors Does It Take to Publish an Article? Trends and Patterns in Political Science." *PS: Political Science & Politics* 31(4): 847–56.

Freese, Jeremy. 2007. "Replication Standards for Quantitative Social Science: Why Not Sociology?" *Sociological Methods and Research* 36: 153–72.

Fujii, Lee Ann. 2012. "Research Ethics 101: Dilemmas and Responsibilities." *PS: Political Science & Politics* 45(4): 717–23.

Garand, James C. 1990. "An Alternative Interpretation of Recent Political Science Journal Evaluations." *PS: Political Science and Politics* 23(September): 448–51.

Garand, James C. 2005. "Integration and Fragmentation in Political Science: Exploring Patterns of Scholarly Communication in a Divided Discipline." *Journal of Politics* 67(4): 979–1005.

Garand, James C., and Micheal W. Giles. 2003. "Journals in the Discipline: A Report on a New Survey of American Political Scientists." *PS: Political Science and Politics* 36(April): 293–308.

Garand, James C., Micheal W. Giles, André Blais, and Iain McLean. 2009. "Political Science Journals in Comparative Perspective: Evaluating Scholarly Journals in the United States, Canada, and the United Kingdom." *PS: Political Science and Politics* 42(October): 695–717.

Gelman, Andrew. 2015. "Fake Study on Changing Attitudes: Sometimes a Claim that is Too Good to be True, isn't." *Monkey Cage/Washington Post.* https://www.washingtonpost.com/news/monkey-cage/wp/2015/05/20/fake-study -on-changing-attitudes-sometimes-a-claim-that-is-too-good-to-be-true-isnt/ ?arc404=true. Accessed October 12, 2020.

Gerber, Alan S., and Donald P. Green. 2000. "The Effects of Canvassing, Telephone Calls, and Direct Mail on Voter Turnout: A Field Experiment." *American Political Science Review* 94(3): 653–63.

Gerber, Alan S., and Donald P. Green. 2005. "Correction to Gerber and Green (2000), Replication of Disputed Findings, and Reply to Imai (2005)." *American Political Science Review* 99(2): 301–13. doi:10.1017/S000305540505166X.

Gerber, Alan S., and Neil Malhotra. 2008. "Do Statistical Reporting Standards Affect What Is Published? Publication Bias in Two Leading Political Science Journals." *Quarterly Journal of Political Science* 3(3): 313–26.

Gerber, Alan S., Neil Malhotra, Conor M. Dowling, and David Doherty. 2010. "Publication Bias in Two Political Behavior Literatures." *American Politics Research* 38(4): 591–613.

Gherghina, Sergiu, and Alexia Katsanidou. 2013. "Data Availability in Political Science Journals." *European Political Science* 12: 333–49.

Gibson, James L. 1995. "Cautious Reflections on a Data Archiving Policy for Political Science." *PS: Political Science and Politics* 28: 473–6.

Giles, Micheal W., and James C. Garand. 2007. "Ranking Political Science Journals: Reputational and Citational Approaches." *PS: Political Science & Politics* 40(4): 741–51.

Gleditsch, Nils Petter. 2012. "Open Access in International Relations: A Symposium." International Studies Perspectives 13(3): 211–15.

Gleditsch, Nils Petter, Claire Metelits, and Håvard Strand. 2003a. "Posting Your Data: Will You Be Scooped or Will You Be Famous?" *International Studies Perspectives* 4: 89–97.

Gleditsch, Nils Petter, Patrick James, James L. Ray, and Bruce Russett. 2003b. "Editors' Joint Statement: Minimum Replication Standards for International Relations Journals." *International Studies Perspectives* 4: 105.

Goodson, Patricia. 2017. *Becoming an Academic Writer*. Thousand Oaks, CA: Sage.

Griffin, Larry, and Charles C. Ragin. 1994. "Formal Methods of Qualitative Analyis." Special issue of *Sociological Methods and Research* 23, 1.

Guardian Staff. 2016. "CV of Failures: Princeton Professor Publishes Resume of His Career Lows." *The Guardian*, April 29. https://www.theguardian.com/education/2016/apr/30/cv-of-failures-princeton-professor-publishes-resume-of-his-career-lows. Accessed 2 May 2020.

Gubler, Joshua R., and Joel S. Selway. 2016. "Considering the Political Consequences of Comparative Politics Experiments," in Scott Desposato (ed.), *Ethics and Experiments: Problems and Solutions for Social Scientists and Policy Professionals*, New York: Routledge, pp. 171–82.

Harzing, Anne-Wil. 2020. "Metrics: H and G-Index." May 26. https://harzing.com/resources/publish-or-perish/tutorial/metrics/h-and-g-index. Accessed May 26, 2020.

Humphreys, Macartan, Raul Sanchez de la Sierra, and Peter van der Windt. 2013. "Fishing, Commitment, and Communication: A Proposal for Comprehensive Nonbinding Research Registration." *Political Analysis* 21(1): 1–20.

ICMJE [International Committee of Medical Journal Editors]. 2020. "Defining the Role of Authors and Contributors." http://www.icmje.org/recommendations/browse/roles-and-responsibilities/defining-the-role-of-authors-and-contributors.html#:~:text=The%20ICMJE%20recommends%20that%20authorship%20be%20based%20on,version%20to%20be%20published%3B%20AND%20More%20items...%20. Accessed October 11, 2020.

Imai, Kosuke. 2005. "Do Get-Out-the-Vote Calls Reduce Turnout? The Importance of Statistical Methods for Field Experiments." *American Political Science Review* 99(2): 283–300.

INASP. n.d. "Journals Online Project." https://www.inasp.info/project/journals-online-project. Accessed June 8, 2020.

Ishiyama, John. 2014. "Replication, Research Transparency, and Journal Publications: Individualism, Community Models, and the Future of Replication Studies." *PS: Political Science & Politics* 47(1): 78–83.

James, Patrick. 2003. "Replication Policies and Practices in International Studies Quarterly." *International Studies Perspectives* 4: 85–8.

Janz, Nicole. 2016. "Bringing the Gold Standard into the Classroom: Replication in University Teaching." *International Studies Perspectives* 17(4): 392–407.

Janz, Nicole, and Jeremy Freese. 2020. "Replicate Others as You Would Like to be Replicated Yourself." *PS: Political Science and Politics.* doi:10.1017/S1049096520000943.

Jensenius, Francesca, Mala Htun, David J. Samuels, David A. Singer, Adria Lawrence, and Michael Chwe. 2018. "The Benefits and Pitfalls of Google Scholar." *PS: Political Science & Politics* 51(4): 820–24.

Jisc [formerly known as Joint Information Systems Committee]. 2019. "An Introduction to Open Access." https://www.jisc.ac.uk/guides/an-introduction -to-open-access. Accessed June 4, 2020.

Jisc [formerly known as Joint Information Systems Committee]. 2020. "Sherpa Romeo." https://v2.sherpa.ac.uk/romeo/search.html. Accessed June 5, 2020.

Jordan, Sara R., and Kim Q. Hill. 2012. "Ethical Assurance Statements in Political Science Journals." *Journal of Academic Ethics* 10(3): 243–50.

Kapiszewski, Diana, and Sebastian Karcher. 2021. "Transparency in Practice in Qualitative Research." *PS: Political Science & Politics*, 54(2), 285–291. doi: 10.1017/S1049096520000955

King, Gary. 1995. "Replication, Replication." *PS: Political Science & Politics* 28(3): 444–52.

King, Gary. 2003. "The Future of the Replication Movement." *International Studies Perspectives* 4: 100–105.

King, Gary. 2006. "Publication, Publication." *PS: Political Science and Politics* 39(1): 119–125.

King, Gary, Emmanuela Gakidou, Kosuke Imai, Jason Lakin, Ryan T. Moore, Clayton Nall, Nirmala Ravishankar, et al. 2009. "Public Policy for the Poor? A Randomized Assessment of the Mexican Universal Health Insurance Programme." *Lancet* 373(9673): 1447–54.

King, Gary, Emmanuela Gakidou, Nirmala Ravishankar, Ryan T. Moore, Jason Lakin, Manett Vargas, Martha Maria Tellez-Rojo, et al. 2007. "A 'Politically Robust' Experimental Design for Public Policy Evaluation, with Application to the Mexican Universal Health Insurance Program." *Journal of Policy Analysis and Management* 26(3): 479–506.

Knott, Eleanor. 2019. "Beyond the Field: Ethics after Fieldwork in Politically Dynamic Contexts." *Perspectives on Politics* 17(1): 140–53.

Laitin, David D. 2013. "Fisheries Management." *Political Analysis* 21(1): 42–7.

Lake, David. 2010. "Who's on First? Listing Authors by Relative Contribution Trumps the Alphabet." *PS: Political Science & Politics* 43(1): 43–7.

Lebo, Matthew J. 2016. "Managing Your Research Pipeline." *PS: Political Science and Politics* 49(2): 259–64.

Levine, Felice J., and Paula R. Skedsvold. 2008. "Where the Rubber Meets the Road: Aligning IRBs and Research Practice." *PS: Political Science and Politics* 41(3): 501–5. doi:10.1017/S1049096508080888.

Lupia, Arthur and George Alter. 2014. "Data Access and Research Transparency in the Quantitative Tradition." *PS: Political Science and Politics* 47(1): 54–9.

Lupia, Arthur and Colin Elman. 2014. "Openness in Political Science: Data Access and Research Transparency." *PS: Political Science and Politics* 47(1): 19–42.

Lupia, Arthur and Colin Elman. 2015. "The Data Access & Research Transparency (DART): A Joint Statement by Political Science Journal Editors." https:// cps.isr.umich.edu/project/the-data-access-research-transparency-dart-a-joint -statement-by-political-science-journal-editors/. Accessed March 2021.

Maliniak, Daniel, Ryan M. Powers, and Barbara F. Walter. 2013. "The Gender Citation Gap in International Relations." *International Organization* 67(4): 889–922.

Martinson, Brian C., Melissa S. Anderson, and Raymond de Vries. 2005. "Scientists Behaving Badly." *Nature* 435: 737–8.

McDermott, Rose, and Peter K. Hatemi. 2010. "Emerging Models of Collaboration in Political Science: Changes, Benefits, and Challenges." *PS: Political Science & Politics* 43(1): 49–58.

McGuire, Kevin T. 2010. "There Was a Crooked Man(uscript): A Not So Serious Look at the Serious Subject of Plagiarism." *PS: Political Science and Politics* 43(1): 107–13.

Mehlum, Halvor. 2012. "The Case for Open Access Publishing." *International Studies Perspectives* 13(3): 216–23.

Merton, Robert K. 1973 [1942]. "The Normative Structure of Science," in Robert K. Merton (ed.), *The Sociology of Science: Theoretical and Empirical Investigations*, Chicago, IL: University of Chicago Press, pp. 267–80.

Miller, Arthur, Tor Wynn, Phil Ullrich, and Mollie Marti. 2001. "Concept and Measurement Artifact in Multiple Values and Value Conflict Models." *Political Research Quarterly* 54(2): 407–19.

Miller, Beth, Jon Pevehouse, Ron Rogowski, Dustin Tingley, and Rick Wilson. 2013. "How to Be a Peer Reviewer: A Guide for Recent and Soon-to-Be PhDs." *PS: Political Science and Politics* 46(1): 120–23.

Mitchell, Sara Mclaughlin, Samantha Lange, and Holly Brus. 2013. "Gendered Citation Patterns in International Relations Journals." *International Studies Perspectives* 14(4): 485–92.

Moher, David, Lex Bouter, Sabine Kleinert, Paul Glasziou, Mai Har Sham, Virginia Barbour, Anne-Marie Coriat, Nicole Foeger, and Ulrich Dirnagl. 2020. "The Hong Kong Principles for Assessing Researchers: Fostering Research Integrity." *PLoS Biology* 18(7): e3000737.

Monogan III, James E. 2013. "A Case for Registering Studies of Political Outcomes: An Application in the 2010 House Elections." *Political Analysis* 21(1): 21–37.

Monogan III, James E. 2015. "Research Preregistration in Political Science: The Case, Counterarguments, and a Response to Critiques." *PS: Political Science & Politics* 48(3): 425–9.

Montgomery, Scott. 2017. "Writing for General, Non-Academic Audiences: Benefits, Opportunities, Issues." September 12. https://jsis.washington.edu/news/writing-general-non-academic-audiences-benefits-opportunities-issues/. Accessed 21 May 2020.

Moravcsik, Andrew. 2019. *Transparency in Qualitative Research* London: Sage.

Moravcsik, Andrew, Colin Elman, and Diana Kapiszewski. 2013. *A Guide to Active Citation*. Qualitative Data Repository (QDR), Center for Qualitative and Multi Method Inquiry (CQMI), Syracuse University. Version 1.8.

Morgan, Cliff, Bob Campbell, and Terri Teleen. 2012. "The Role of the Academic Journal Publisher and Open Access Publishing Models." *International Studies Perspectives* 13(3): 228–34.

Nentwich, Michael. 2008. "Political Science on the Web: Prospects and Challenges." *European Political Science* 7(2): 220–29.

Nissani, Moti. 1990. "A Cognitive Reinterpretation of Stanley Milgram's Observations on Obedience to Authority." *American Psychologist* 45(12): 1384–5.

OASPA [Open Access Scholarly Publishers Association]. 2020. https://oaspa.org/. Accessed June 8, 2020.

OHRP [Office for Human Research Protections]. 2018. "Listing of Social-Behavioral Research Standards." https://www.hhs.gov/ohrp/international/social-behavioral-research-standards/index.html. Accessed October 21, 2020.

ORI [Office of Research Integrity]. n.d. "Definition of Research Misconduct." https://ori.hhs.gov/definition-misconduct. Accessed October 11, 2020.

Peffley, Mark, Pia Knigge, and Jon Hurwitz. 2001a. "A Multiple Values Model of Political Tolerance." *Political Research Quarterly* 54(2): 379–406.

Peffley, Mark, Pia Knigge, and Jon Hurwitz. 2001b. "A Reply to Miller et al.: Replication Made Simple." *Political Research Quarterly* 54(2): 421–9.

Phillips, Brian J. 2014. "Ranking IR Journals." Duck of Minerva. January 7. https://duckofminerva.com/2014/01/ranking-ir-journals.html. Accessed 22 October 2019.

Polsky, Andrew J. 2007. "Seeing Your Name in Print: Unpacking the Mysteries of the Review Process at Political Science Scholarly Journals." *PS: Political Science & Politics* 40(3): 539–43.

Powner, Leanne C. 2015. *Empirical Research and Writing: A Political Science Student's Practical Guide*. Los Angeles, CA: Sage/CQ Press.

Publons. n.d. "Learn to Peer Review with Confidence." https://publons.com/community/academy/. Accessed May 20, 2020.

Publons. 2018. *Global State of Peer Review*. Publons/Web of Science Group.

Retraction Watch. n.d. "Retraction Watch Database User Guide Appendix B: Reasons." https://retractionwatch.com/retraction-watch-database-user-guide/retraction-watch-database-user-guide-appendix-b-reasons/. Accessed October 16, 2020.

Rich, Timothy S. 2013. "Publishing as a Graduate Student: A Quick and (Hopefully) Painless Guide to Establishing Yourself as a Scholar." *PS: Political Science & Politics* 46(2): 376–9.

Rich, Timothy S. 2016. "Predatory Publishing, Open Access, and the Costs to Academia." *PS: Political Science & Politics* 49(2): 265–7.

Roig, Miguel. 2015. "Avoiding Plagiarism, Self-Plagiarism, and Other Questionable Writing Practices: A Guide to Ethical Writing." Office of Research Integrity, US Department of Health and Human Services. https://ori.hhs.gov/avoiding-plagiarism-self-plagiarism-and-other-questionable-writing-practices-guide-ethical-writing. Accessed September 23, 2020.

Roselle, Laura, and Sharon Spray. 2016. *Research and Writing in International Relations*. New York: Routledge.

Samuels, David J. 2011. "The Modal Number of Citations to Political Science Articles Is Greater than Zero: Accounting for Citations in Articles and Books." *PS: Political Science & Politics* 44(4): 783–92.

Schwartz-Shea, Peregrine, and Dvora Yanow. 2016. "Legitimizing Political Science or Splitting the Discipline? Reflections on DA-RT and the Policy-making Role of a Professional Association." *Politics and Gender* E 11. doi:https://doi.org/10.1017/S1743923X16000428.

Seligson, Mitchell A. 2016. "Human Subjects Research Protection and Large-N Research," in Scott Desposato (ed.), *Ethics and Experiments: Problems and Solutions for Social Scientists and Policy Professionals*, New York: Routledge, pp. 241–54.

Sigelman, Lee. 2009. "Are Two (or Three or Four ... or Nine) Heads Better than One? Collaboration, Multidisciplinarity, and Publishability." *PS: Political Science & Politics* 42(3): 507–12.

Simon, Rita J., Von Bakanic, and Clark McPhail. 1986. "Who Complains to Journal Editors and What Happens." *Sociological Inquiry* 56(2): 259–71.

Singal, Jesse. 2015. "The Case of the Amazing Gay-Marriage Data: How a Graduate Student Reluctantly Uncovered a Huge Scientific Fraud." *New York Magazine*, May 29. https://www.thecut.com/2015/05/how-a-grad-student-uncovered-a-huge-fraud.html. Accessed October 14, 2020.

Stop Predatory Journals. n.d. https://predatoryjournals.com. Accessed June 8, 2020.

The Belmont Report [United States Department of Health, Education, and Welfare (HEW), Office of the Secretary]. 1979. https://www.hhs.gov/ohrp/sites/default/files/the-belmont-report-508c_FINAL.pdf. Accessed October 11, 2020.

Think, Check, Submit. 2020. https://thinkchecksubmit.org/. Accessed June 8, 2020.

Thompson, William R. 2012. "Why Journal Editors Have Other and More Pressing Concerns." *International Studies Perspectives* 13(3): 224–7.

Thunder, David. 2004. "Back to Basics: Twelve Rules for Writing a Publishable Article." *PS: Political Science & Politics* 37(3): 493–5.

Tijdink, Joeri K., Reinout Verbeke, and Yvo M. Smulders. 2014. "Publication Pressure and Scientific Misconduct in Medical Scientists." *Journal of Empirical Research on Human Research Ethics* 9(5): 64–71.

Ulrich's Global Serials Directory. 2020. https://ulrichsweb.com/.

United States Holocaust Memorial Museum [USHMM]. 2020. "Nuremburg Code." https://www.ushmm.org/information/exhibitions/online-exhibitions/special-focus/doctors-trial/nuremberg-code. Accessed October 17, 2020.

Van Cott, Donna Lee. 2005. "A Graduate Student's Guide to Publishing Scholarly Journal Articles." *PS: Political Science & Politics* 38(4): 741–3.

Van Noorden, Richard. 2015. "Political Science's Problem with Research Ethics." *Nature News & Comment.* http://www.nature.com/news/political-science-s-problem-with-research-ethics-1.17866. Accessed October 12, 2020.

WCRIF [World Conferences on Research Integrity Foundation]. 2020. "Mission." https://wcrif.org/foundation/mission. Accessed October 14, 2020.

Weeks, Gregory. 2006. "Facing Failure: The Use (and Abuse) of Rejection in Political Science." *PS: Political Science & Politics* 39(4): 879–82.

Wilkinson, Jo. 2020. "Want to Peer Review? Top 10 Tips to Get Noticed by Editors." Blog.publons.com, January 8. https://publons.com/blog/10-things-you-need-to-know-to-get-noticed-by-editors/. Accessed January 29, 2020.

Williams, Ann E. 2017. "Altmetrics: An Overview and Evaluation." *Online Information Review* 41(3): 311–17.

Willis, Derek. 2014. "Professors' Research Project Stirs Political Outrage in Montana." *New York Times.* https://www.nytimes.com/2014/10/29/upshot/professors-research-project-stirs-political-outrage-in-montana.html. Accessed October 12, 2020.

Wilson, Rick K., William Mischler, and John Ishiyama. 2016. "Journal Editors as Ethics Sheriffs," in Scott Desposato (ed.), *Ethics and Experiments: Problems and Solutions for Social Scientists and Policy Professionals*, New York: Routledge, pp. 262–6.

Zigerell, L. J. 2013. "Rookie Mistakes: Preemptive Comments on Graduate Student Empirical Research Manuscripts." *PS: Political Science & Politics* 46(1): 142–6.

Index